THE ORIGINAL METS, The Metropolitan Police

The Police of New York City

robert l. bryan

Published by robert l. bryan, 2023.

While every precaution has been taken in the preparation of this book, the publisher assumes no responsibility for errors or omissions, or for damages resulting from the use of the information contained herein.

THE ORIGINAL METS, THE METROPOLITAN POLICE

First edition. August 10, 2023.

ISBN: 979-8223163954

Written by robert l. bryan.

For Meghan - Always the Angel on my Shoulder.

PROLOGUE

There is some controversy regarding whether baseball originated in the United States. Abner Doubleday may not have invented baseball, and perhaps baseball is the distant cousin of the English game of rounders. Still, baseball soon became an essential part of the American identity. While other sports were enjoyed by many, the sport of baseball became a sport that unified all people. It became a common ground for the ethnically and religiously diverse people of America.

Everyone could enjoy baseball. No matter who they were, where they came from, or what they believed in, everyone could enjoy watching, playing, and talking about baseball. As a result, baseball is not only a popular sport to watch, but also a very popular sport to play. Baseball has not only played a part in American history, but also the personal lives of the American people. It truly became the National Pastime.

Baseball could also be called New York City's pastime. Many American cities dream of having one major league team, but for over fifty years three teams slugged it out within the confines of New York City. When the Dodgers and Giants broke the heart of the city after the 1957 season by pulling up stakes and moving to the west coast, even the mighty Yankees could not fill the void left by their departure. It took just four years for a National League team to join the Yankees in New York City.

Back in 1961, team owner Joan Payson received approval to create the Mets as a replacement for the departed Brooklyn Dodgers and New York Giants in a city suddenly devoid of National League baseball. While the team was still in its nascent stage, it operated under the corporate name "The New York Metropolitan Baseball Club Inc.," which then needed to pick a nickname for the playing field. Payson chose "Mets" for several reasons, one of the reasons being historical in nature. The name harkened back to the Metropolitans, an independent baseball team that eventually became part of the 19th-century American Association and played at the site of what would become the Polo Grounds from 1883 to 1887. The name "Metropolitans" was also used by a yachting team that received coverage by the New York Times in the 1850s.

There was another team of New York City Metropolitans that came into existence shortly after the yachting team began navigating the rivers surrounding the city and disbanded a few years before the baseball team took the field – The New York Metropolitan Police department. This is their story.

CHAPTER 1: BEFORE THE METS

Policing had not changed very much in New York City since the watch system had been employed. As the city grew, however, in both population and industry, the necessity for a new approach to policing the city began forcing itself on the public mind.

By the time the Revolutionary War ended, the city's population had grown to 60,000 - and police protection had become a major problem. But little was done to deal with it. Crime continued to increase through the late 1820's. Although more watchmen were hired, they were widely regarded as incompetent and the protection they provided was considered inadequate. For years the situation remained this way. Nothing was done until contempt for the city's weak police force finally gave way to fear – fear that the city's social disintegration was imminent. And with that fear came the realization that something had to be done about providing New York with a strong, effective police department.

However apparent the need for change might have been to the politicians of the time, they had neither the will nor inclination to change the old way of doing business. And so, the status quo of policing dragged along until 1840. At that time the city was enjoying growing industrial prosperity and George W. Matsell became one of the Police Magistrates. He was a young man of talent and considerable energy, and most importantly, he recognized the necessity for a change in the watch system, and he set himself to reorganize the old sleepy Leatherheads, the nickname for the watchmen of the period.

During the mid-1800's, New York became home to thousands of destitute and desperate immigrants from Ireland and Germany. Many could barely afford housing in the rat-infested, unlit, unheated and horribly overcrowded tenements and wooden shanties on the city's outskirts. Salaries at the time scarcely provided working people with enough to cover their living expenses. Men, women, and children as young as ten earned less than 30-cents a day for laboring 12 to 15 hours in unhealthy and hazardous factories. City streets were unpaved, lacked proper drainage, and were cluttered with uncollected trash. When it rained, they quickly became quagmires of mud and filth. Many people fell sick from contaminated water, and overcrowded living conditions caused disease to spread rapidly and uncontrollably. Crime was rampant on the unlit streets, especially when moonless nights left large parts of the city in total darkness. It was common for thieves to roam the streets burglarizing buildings and attacking people as they hurried home. Living conditions, such as these, caused anger and despair, making New York fertile ground for a tremendous growth in crime, vice and disorder.

The crime rose with the population, which had reached about 400,000. Matsell gathered some kindred spirits about him, and, with the squad of men he had at his command, he was in the habit of going about the city at night, breaking up the criminal activities. Matsell's efforts showed what one earnest, fearless man, could accomplish, and the public mind became impressed with what he was doing, prompting public pressure to change the system of policing. No action was taken, however, until James Harper was elected Mayor in 1844, but once action was initiated there was no turning back on police progress and reform.

The Municipal Police Act was passed in the year 1844, and George Matsell became Chief of Police. For twelve years he occupied the position, gradually improving the police system and enforcing strict discipline. It was Matsell who originated the much-quoted phrase, " the finest police force in the world."

The Police system was clearly approaching a turning point in its history. Sweeping and radical changes were taking place. The system of policing the city that had prevailed, with few changes and modifications, as handed down from the Dutch to the English, and by these to the government of the United States City of New York, was legislated out of existence on May 7, 1844. Prior to that time the police force of the city consisted of two constables elected annually in each ward, of a small body of marshals appointed by the mayor, and of a night watch composed of citizens who pursued their trades during the day and patrolled the streets at night. This act abolished the night watch and established a Day and Night Police.

The officers and annual salaries were as follows:

Captains: $1250

Assistant Captains: $700

Sergeants: $600

Policemen: $500

The mayor was authorized to prescribe a distinguishing badge or dress for the members of the force, and also to prescribe such rules and regulations as he might deem necessary and proper. With these radical changes being made to New York City, the mayor and politicians needed a strong, effective model to copy. They decided on the Metropolitan Police of London.

In 1828, Sir Robert Peel, British Home Secretary, introduced a bill establishing a paid professional police force - one that wore uniforms, was well drilled and devoted itself full-time to protecting the peace. Nicknamed "bobbies" and "peelers," this police force had been created because of a marked increase in criminal activity in England. With a similar upsurge in crime in their own city, New Yorkers decided to try a similar solution.

Mayor James Harper ordered that after a certain date the men going out on patrol should wear a uniform, then being designed, but this order brought about a revolt among the policemen.

Mr. James W. Gerard, a rich young police buff with a love for almost anything regarding England had just returned from a visit to London. Sir Robert Peel, the head of the police force of London, had just introduced a police uniform for the men on patrol, and Gerard noted the lack of rowdyism and crime on the streets of London, and attributed this condition, at least in part, to the uniform worn by the London Police. Upon his return to New York, he called upon Mayor Harper and recommended a similar uniform for the police of New York City.

Mayor Harper quickly went to work to uniform, or partially uniform, the corps of two hundred men which constituted the Municipal Police. This uniform consisted of a blue single- breasted cloth frock coat, buttoned to the neck, having the letters M. P. on a standing collar. This was the first serious attempt made to uniform the police force. Policemen were variously called " M. P's." and " Harper's Police. "

Many policemen strongly objected to wearing a specially designed uniform, preferring to dress in their own clothes. They viewed the uniform as a British innovation and an infringement on their rights as freeborn American citizens. Many citizens shared this contempt and publicly condemned a uniform force as nothing more than a "standing army" and "liveried lackeys."

After wearing this uniform for some time, the men got tired of having the people call them the Harper's Police, or the M. P.'s. They refused to wear the uniform any longer as they did not want to be a second edition of the London Bobby, or a butler in some household. Police Inspector Thorne, a favorite among the men, was instructed to use his influence with them, but he could not convince them of the virtue of wearing the uniform. The men were holding meetings of protest in Military Hall on the Bowery, and elsewhere. But after some three or more weeks, Inspector Thorne told the men that if they would not wear the uniform on the next tour of duty, he would withdraw from the case and the men would be dismissed. But before leaving the Inspector said to them, "My good men, we have worked in harmony for a long while, and it will hurt me to see you lose your jobs, so for my sake and the sake of your families consider your positions."

The policemen took a vote and concluded to take Inspector Thorne's advice and don the uniform. Police officers wore an eight-point, star-shaped copper badge over the left breast of their coats and became known as "star police" and later on as "coppers" and "cops."

The State Legislature authorized the hiring of up to 800 men. But the City Council, rather than adopting the concept, decided that it could get by with a municipal police force of only 200 men. This small force, of course, quickly proved inadequate. In 1845, the original act of the State Legislature was adopted and a uniformed Municipal Police Force of 800 men was established. The Chief held office for four years, unless sooner removed for cause. Policemen were ap pointed to office for two years.

Despite all the changes to policing, the system was not running smoothly. Corruption was running rampant and Mayor Brady, in his annual message, May 11, 1847, stated that the new police system had failed to meet the just expectations of the community, and recommended to the Common Council the propriety of urging the legislature to abolish the current Police force which afforded so little protection to citizens and their property, more especially at night, and suggested the advisability of the establishment of a night-watch to consist of 1,200 men, or a virtual return to the old watch system.

The first set of printed rules and regulations issued to the force was in September, 1848. They were drafted by Chief Matsell and William McKellar, who was Matsell's chief clerk, and, generally speaking, his guide, philosopher and friend. These rules and regulations made up a handy little book of about ninety pages. When issued, it was received with amazement and alarm by the men. The inscription on the fly leaf of one of these books, evidently written by the particular policeman to whom it originally belonged, read as follows: " A policeman would not live one year if he acted up to these regulations. " This sentiment voiced the opinion of the whole force whom the book was designed to instruct in their duties.

The instructions required each member of the department to wear the emblem of his office on the outside of the outermost garment over the left breast. Members of the force should, when on duty, conspicuously display their star (shield) or emblem of office. The captain of each patrol district divided the policemen of his district into two equal parts, to be known as the first and second platoon, which were commanded respectively by the first and second assistant captains. The captain also divided his district into night and day beats and designated the policemen who were to patrol the same; and, in like manner, established two or more day stations, in order that citizens might at all times during the day obtain the aid of policemen when needed.

The rule book emphasized that the prevention of crime was the most important object of the policeman's job, and that the rules should be maintained to accomplish that end; and by his vigilance, to render it extremely difficult for anyone to commit crime on his beat.

It was admitted by all that the force at this time was a long way from being "the finest in the world. " An opinion prevailed that it would have been far better for the public at large to have left things as they had been. In fact, as illustrated in the mayor's address, there was a cry for a return to the old watch system.

Chief Matsell came to the forefront as the biggest advocate for the new system of policing. He quoted figures to prove that while the old night-watch employed more men, they did not afford as good police protection as the force that had succeeded it. But this did not diminish the popular discontent, and the cry continued for a change in the law. The next Mayor, Havemeyer, in his annual message, stated, "the defect which was most prominent in the system was the appointment of policemen for a single year."

With their term of office being the same as an aldermen, and others responsible for appointing them, there was danger, the mayor thought, that the whole system would be involved in the incessant confusion resulting from annual changes of parties, with the policemen precluded from gaining experience and independence which were indispensable to their usefulness. Acting upon the mayor's suggestions, the Committee on Police pushed the legislature to amend the Police Acts by abolishing one or two year police employment and instead making the length of employment indeterminate and based on good behavior.

Full uniforms were finally adopted in 1853. The first full uniform consisted of a leather helmet and a blue, single-breasted cloth frock coat, buttoned to the neck with the letters M.P. (Municipal Police) on a standing collar. Gray trousers, with a half-inch black stripe running down the side of each leg, completed the outfit. Each officer was equipped with a baton that was 22 inches long and three-quarters of an inch thick. The Department "Rules and Regulations" required that the club be used only "in urgent self-defense." The Municipal Police were not authorized to carry side arms for patrol duty.

Formal training came into existence in 1853. Police captains instructed officers in the "school of soldier" and drill instructors were appointed to train and discipline officers in crowd and riot control.

During the early 1850's, the New York Police constructed a simple telegraph network between their chief's office and the various precincts. The primary purpose of this communications system was to speed the dispatch of extra officers to fire and riot scenes. However, most of the messages dealt with lost children and stray horses.

The Act of 1844, as has been said, abolished the watch system. In lieu of the Watch Department, marshals, street Inspectors, Health wardens, fire wardens, dock masters, lamp- lighters, bell ringers, inspectors of pawnbrokers and junk- shops, and of the officers to attend the polls, there was established a Day and Night Police, not to exceed eight hundred men, including captains, assistant captains and policemen. Each ward was constituted a patrol district, in each of which there was established a district headquarters. In addition to their other duties, the law obliged policemen to light the lamps and ring the alarm bells.

The chief of police, subordinate to the mayor, was the chief executive officer. His office was located at City Hall, in the mayor's office. He was appointed by the mayor, by and with the consent of the Common Council, to serve for one year, unless sooner removed. The aldermen, assistant aldermen, and assessors of each Ward, with the concurrence of the mayor, were empowered to appoint a captain, one first assistant captain, one second assistant captain, and as many policemen as the ward was entitled to, whose term of office was also for one year.

The legislature also raised the level of the police force to a maximum not to exceed 900 men, and the rank of sergeant was created. A patrol district was established in each ward, where a suitable room was maintained for the use of such patrol, the name of this room being changed from district headquarters to "Police Station House." The patrol of each district consisted of one captain, a first and second assistant captain, two or more sergeants, and such number of policemen as the Common Council should apportion to the ward or district. The captains of the several wards nominated to the aldermen and assistant aldermen of their wards suitable policemen to perform the duties of sergeants, not exceeding four or less than two for each.

Some of the most important changes effected by the charter of 1853 consisted of abolishing the Board of Assistant Aldermen and substituting instead, a Board of Councilmen, consisting of sixty members, one to be elected from each of sixty districts of contiguous territory; and the appointment of the mayor, recorder, and city judge as a Board of Commissioners, by whom the officers of the police and policemen were thereafter to be appointed. The Police Department was made to consist of the following named officers: Chief of Police, Captains, Lieutenants, Sergeants, Policemen, and Doormen. The Charter memorialized that police officers appointed after the passage of this Act were to hold office during good behavior and could be removed only for cause. The Chief and Captains were empowered to suspend Sergeants, Policemen, and Doormen, for cause, in manner prescribed by Act of 1846.

The qualifications and method of appointment to the police department was as follows: The law required that a policeman should be a United States citizen, and a resident of the ward; should read and write; and understand the first four rules of arithmetic (addition, subtraction, multiplication, and division); and bear a good character for honesty, morality, and sobriety.

Previous to appointment he was required to present to the mayor a certificate signed by twenty-five reputable citizens, two-thirds of whom should be residents of his own Ward, to the effect that they had known him for five years, and that his character came up to the required official standard. He was likewise obliged to present to the mayor a surgeon's certificate that he was of sound body and robust constitution.

The effective force on the first day of July 1853, was:

20 Captains

40 Lieutenants

79 Sergeants

864 Policemen,

1003 Total.

The condition and efficiency of the police department, it was acknowledged, had materially improved since the foregoing Act of the legislature went into operation. Among the important changes thereby brought about were the tenure of office, which was limited only to the good behavior of the incumbent. The power of appointment was vested in a commission, consisting of the recorder, city judge, and mayor, who had the sole power to try and punish parties violating the rules of the department, and who, in conjunction with the chief of police, were authorized to prescribe rules for the government of the force.

The greatest benefit resulting to the community under the law of 1853, was the separation of the department from political influences. Under the former law, policemen well understood that they had to enter the political arena and connect themselves with the dominant political party in the separate wards, in order to secure a re-appointment at the expiration of the term for which they were appointed. Instead of being disinterested officers at the polls during the election, they became interested partisans, striving for the success of their favorite candidates. Policemen were found connected with clubs, committees, and other organizations of a political character, leading them to perform their duty with inattention, and sometimes to entirely neglect it, thus exercising a most baneful influence upon the efficiency and character of the department. In this way the whole force was turned into a political engine for the advancement of particular parties or individuals. To obviate this evil, the commissioners adopted a rule to the effect that no member would be permitted to connect himself, directly or indirectly, in any way, with a society, club, committee, or organization of any kind, the object of which was the political advancement of a party or individual.

There was a large increase in the number of arrests that Chief Matsell claimed, resulted from an increased activity and vigilance on the part of policemen. The force, without doubt, had greatly improved. The appointment of commissioners and the introduction of a uniform had much to do with this. A stricter discipline was also enforced, and the men began to take an honest pride in their work.

Watchman's Hat.

Old Leatherhead and Sentry Box.

Chief Matsell's Shield.

London Metropolitan Police "Peeler"
The inspiration for the first New York Police uniform

Mayor Harper.

Police Captain's Shield.
(Star Police.)

Police captains - 1856

CHAPTER 2: MEET THE METS

The general feeling was that the police department and the city were on the right track. Then, in 1854, New York elected a new mayor, Fernando Wood, the first of the big-city political bosses who would flourish in America over the next hundred years. Born in Philadelphia in 1812, Wood came to New York with his family and went into the liquor and cigar business as a young man. In 1840 he was elected to Congress with Tammany Hall backing. After losing his first race for mayor in 1850, he was careful to obtain the backing of the most influential leaders of the city's organized crime.

Wood was a charmer. Early in his reign he mounted a number of high-profile initiatives that helped him gain the backing of New York's most influential citizens and politicians. Responding to the growing complaints about carriage and omnibus traffic on the nation's most famous shopping boulevard, he created a "Broadway Squad" of tall, handsome policemen who stood ready to help nervous citizens make the difficult crossing. Wood also inspired the annual police parade which remained a great civic event for the next 75-years. The dashing mayor personally led the police in closing saloons on Sunday and chasing prostitutes from the streets. But his more serious innovations had to do with getting votes and collecting graft. He was the first city leader to appreciate the full value of the police in both these areas and to efficiently organize them to serve the interests of the political machine.

Wood was not subtle. While his predecessors had tried to maintain a certain veneer of respectability, he openly ran city government to benefit himself and his Tammany Hall cohorts. It was also in this period that the police department's possibilities as a vessel of political patronage came to be fully appreciated. In an administration that relied on saloonkeepers, gangs, and "shoulder-hitters" to manage elections, it was only natural for the police to draw on the same general pool of talent. Under Wood, the force took in men who were described as "five foot nothing" with names like "English Bill" and "Dutch Pete." Mike Murray, a saloon brawler, was appointed directly from civilian life as a captain in the First District. It was during Wood's reign that the police department began to take on an Irish flavor. He was the first mayor to mobilize the immigrant vote on a grand scale.

In 1856, the public opinion turned sharply against Wood after an election campaign in which he won a second term with the conspicuous help of the Dead Rabbits gang as well as the police. The following January, the newly elected governor of New York, John King – a republican – proposed an ingenious measure to pull the rug out from under Wood and his associates. The state would create a Metropolitan Police District to Include New York City, Kings County (Brooklyn), Westchester County, and Richmond County (Staten Island). Of course, the real target of the legislation was New York City and its 750,000 residents. Westchester and Richmond counties were rural, and the policing of Brooklyn's 250,000 inhabitants had not yet become a problem.

With the passage of the Metropolitan Police Act in 1857, a Metropolitan Police District was created, and a Board of Commissioners was instituted, to be appointed for five years by the governor of the state, to have the sole control of the appointment, trial, and management of the police force, which was not to outnumber two thousand, and to appoint the chief of police and the minor offices.

The Governor appointed five Commissioners of Police; one from the county of Richmond or Westchester, one from Kings County, and three from New York, the mayors of New York and Brooklyn being ex-officio members of the Board. The officers of the Board were a president and a treasurer, the Board being empowered to appoint a chief clerk and six deputy clerks. The police force was then made to consist of a general superintendent, two deputy superintendents, five surgeons, inspectors and captains not to exceed forty, sergeants not to exceed one hundred and fifty, and as many patrolmen as should be determined by the Board of Supervisors of New York, the Common Council of Brooklyn, and the Supervisors of the Counties of Kings, Richmond and Westchester.

The qualifications for appointment on the force were about the same as in the preceding Act, with the one and two year appointments eliminated. The salaries were as follows:

Treasurer of the Board: $3,000 per annum

Commissioners: $8 per day, for actual service performed

General Superintendent: $3,000 per annum

Deputy Superintendents: $2,000 per annum

Surgeons: $1,500 per annum

Inspectors and Captains: $1,200 per annum

Sergeants: $900 per annum

Patrolmen: $800 per annum

Doormen: $700 per annum

The chiefs of police, in the cities of New York and Brooklyn, were designated, respectively, deputy superintendents of police. From and after the passage of the Act, captains were designated inspectors and captains. Lieutenants and assistant captains were designated as sergeants, and policemen were designated as patrolmen.

The police districts were divided into precincts, without any regard to county or ward boundaries, with one inspector, one captain, and four sergeants (besides such quota of patrolmen to be thereafter determined) in each precinct. The Board was authorized to establish, from time to time, a station or sub-station in each district for the accommodation of the police force on duty therein. The Board could also detail police officers to the police and criminal courts, public offices of the cities of New York and Brooklyn, the Quarantine and Emigration offices, and other locations as might be deemed advisable. The Board was restrained from suspending members of the force from pay for more than thirty days. All orders and regulations of the Board were promulgated through the general superintendent, who was the head and chief of the police force.

Simeon Draper, James Bowen, James W. Nye, Jacob Cholwell and James S. T. Stranahan were the first appointed commissioners of the Metropolitan Police Board.

Draper, Nye and Cholwell resigned, and Pelatiah Perit and S. B. Ward were appointed their successors. They in turn resigned, and Thomas B. Stillman, Michael Ulshoffer and Isaac H. Bailey were the next appointees. This resulted in the formation of the following Board of Police: James Bowen, of Westchester County; James S. T. Stranahan, of Kings County, Thomas B. Stillman, Michael Ulshoffer and Isaac H. Bailey, of New York.

The Police Commissioners successively appointed the following as General Superintendent: James R. Whitney, Joseph Keene and Welcome R. Beebe, all of whom in turn declined to serve. The Board next appointed Frederick A. Tallmadge, who accepted. Tallmadge served from May 13, 1857 until April 18, 1859. Amos Pilsbury was appointed on May 20, 1859 but did not assume the office of general superintendent until July 1st. Deputy Superintendent Daniel Carpenter was the acting general superintendent until Pilsbury took office and returned to the general superintendent's role when Pilsbury resigned on March 5, 1860.

The Act declared that the Municipal or local police of the cities of New York and Brooklyn should be embodied in the Metropolitan force, and that the local authorities should be divested of all control over them after the first meeting of the Board of Commissioners.

This situation was not to Mayor Wood's liking at all. Officially, he asserted that the state was usurping the condition of home rule that a municipality should have over its police services. Wood considered the power exercised by the State Legislature, in respect to the Act of establishing a Metropolitan Police District, an attempt to usurp his authority, on the ground that the government of the police was entrusted to a Board of Commissioners not appointed or selected by those who were taxed for their salaries, and who were immediately affected by the operation of those laws. The mayor also thought it decidedly objectionable that the state government, besides creating the Board and appointing its officers, should have also fixed their compensation to be paid out of the city treasury, without a right on the part of the people of the city to regulate or control them in any degree.

The mayor said he considered the police an army for preserving domestic order in time of peace, just as the regular army protects the citizens from foreign invasion in time of war. "It should be our object, " he said, "to elevate the guardians of our lives and property to a position of dignity scarcely inferior to the guardians of the national honor." He therefore recommended that the police, in the designation of its men and officers, and also in their appointment, suspension, trial and removal, should be organized and governed according to like features in our military system, the mayor to be considered the head of the force.

Unofficially, Wood was furious at the prospect of losing control of the police, and thereby losing control of much of his ability to control elections and extort graft. Wood fought back immediately against the Metropolitan Police Act by stating confidently that the courts would declare it unconstitutional. The mayor's confidence infused into the minds of members of the New York force questions as to the legality of obeying the orders of the new commissioners. Under these circumstances, and in view of the fact that it was a question of vital importance to the policemen, the Board refrained from assuming the control of the force until the validity of the law was judicially determined. On the May 4, 1857 Justice Clarke, of the Supreme Court, affirmed the constitutionality of the Act, and May 25th the Supreme Court, at general term, declared it valid and binding in all parts.

Once the Supreme Court decisions were rendered the commissioners assumed the direct control of the police force. That portion of the new district in the City of Brooklyn, with but few exceptions, obeyed the orders of the Board. In the New York force, however, fifteen captains and about eight hundred patrolmen refused to recognize the authority of the commissioners or obey the orders of the general superintendent. Charges of insubordination were preferred against them, and they were tried and dismissed from the service in conformity with the provisions of the law. There was some degree of leniency observed by the commissioners. For example, on June 9th, sixty policemen were scheduled to be tried for insubordination. Only two appeared for trial, and the charges for these two officers were dismissed with their promise to support the Metropolitan Police.

— Mayor Fernando Wood

METROPOLITAN POLICE HEAD QUARTERS, MULBERRY STREET NEAR BLEECKER ST

THE LOST FOUND—A SCENE AT THE POLICE HEAD-QUARTERS, MULBERRY STREET, NEW YORK.

Police review on the Battery 1859

CHAPTER 3: COP VS. COP

From 1795 to 1798, yellow fever killed thousands in New York City. In reaction, the New York City Common Council passed a quarantine law in 1799 which funded the creation of the New York Marine Hospital. The hospital had the capacity to house 1,500 patients. At its peak in the 1840s, the quarantine hospital treated more than 8,000 patients each year. By the 1850s a rigorous inspection system was in place. Newly arrived ships were boarded, and if any signs of disease were found, all passengers were unloaded at the quarantine hospital.

The quarantine hospital was on Staten Island (Richmond County) on a large site in the former town of Castleton, overlooking Upper New York Bay near the border of today's St. George and Tompkinsville.

Opposition to the hospital by local residents began from its creation. In this sense, "the quarantine war" could be understood as a decades-long campaign by Staten Islanders against the facility. Landowners opposed the acquisition of the site by the city but also complained about the effects of the Quarantine on property values.

In 1857 New York City officials attempted to defuse local anger by moving the facility to a more remote location on Staten Island, Seguine Point. However, arsonists from the town of Westfield destroyed the construction site before the new facility could be finished. One participant in that attack wrote an anonymous letter to The New York Times, signed as "An Oysterman", warning of further action if construction resumed.

Based on the continued threats, on May 14th, 1857, Deputy Superintendent Matsell was directed to detail five patrolmen to guard the public hospitals at the Quarantine from the threatened attacks of incendiaries. He refused to obey the order and was tried and removed from office for insubordination, and Daniel Carpenter was appointed in his place. Matsell's termination was akin to setting a fuse to dynamite. I would only take a small spark to cause the explosion.

The new Metropolitan Police force, handicapped as they were by the action of the old Municipal Police, and legal proceedings, found their hands full in combating public outbreaks and riotous disturbances, as well as open brawls that ignited between the Metropolitans and the Municipals who refused to recognize the Metropolitan's authority. After exhausting all the resources of the law to evade obedience to the Act, the mayor and municipal government finally caused it to be referred to the Court of Appeals. Before the final decision came, however, that one small spark resulted in the explosion and subsequent spilling of blood.

On June 16th, 1857, the center of Manhattan exploded into chaos. The source of the explosion was a political stand-off between state and city using New York's police against themselves. The subsequent fall out led to a summer of violence and crime, including the legendary Dead Rabbits Riot. The direct incident that led to the police riot was—of all things—an argument over who could appoint the next street commissioner.

Daniel D. Conover, born in 1822, was an American public servant, political activist and industrialist. He was the first to invest in land development on Long Island and, through his efforts, was partly responsible for transforming the southern coastline, then known as the Great South Bay, as a popular summer resort for many prominent New York and Brooklyn families throughout the mid-to late 19th century. But in 1857, Conover had his sights set on another position.

In June of 1857, NYC's Street Commissioner Joseph S.Taylor passed away. Governor John King appointed Daniel Conover, but Mayor Wood appointed Charles Devlin, a contractor and bondsman with strong connections to Wood. Though the mayor and governor had originally agreed on Conover, Wood changed his mind and gave Devlin the appointment. It was rumored that Devlin paid $50,000 for the seat. It was also rumored that Conover was incensed because he had already either offered or given Wood a bribe for the position. $50,000 is a large sum of money today. Why would anyone consider paying that enormous amount of money in 1857 for appointment as street commissioner? The answer is simple – money! Street commissioner was a plum appointment as it related to the potential for graft. Bribes could be solicited from construction companies, water companies, and businesses for not cleaning their sidewalks, just to name a few.

The situation immediately erupted into a scandal, with the state declaring that Wood had no right to appoint Devlin. As a matter of fact, Mayor Wood would have preferred to take the simplest path and appoint the current Deputy Superintendent, Charles Turner, as street commissioner, but Turner had no money to pay a bribe.

Conditions began to boil over on Saturday, June 13th. Daniel Conover made an appearance at the street commissioner's office in the Hall of Records. He had in his possession a piece of paper signed by Governor King appointing him street Commissioner to replace the recently deceased Joseph S. Taylor. Mr. Charles Turner, the deputy superintendent, was taken by surprise, saying he knew nothing of Conover's appointment and admitting that he believed he had assumed the role of commissioner after Taylor's death. As the debate continued peacefully Alderman Clancy arrived with an escort of a squad of Municipal policemen. Clancy said he was acting in his role as president of the aldermen when he authorized Turner to continue to act as street commissioner until furth notice.

Conover voiced disagreement with Clancy's ruling, at which point the alderman turned back the lapel of his coat, revealing the star of a magistrate. Clancy warned Conover to keep himself collected and peaceful or suffer an arrest. Mr. Turner remained in the office until the normal hour of 6PM, at which time he locked the office and went home.

When the street commissioner's office opened on Monday morning June 15th, the controversy continued. When the office opened a squad of twenty Metropolitan Police under Captain Speight and fifteen Municipals under Officer Masterson were sent to the office by their respective police boards. As time passed each force was augmented until the Municipals had swelled to 150 and the Metropolitans 50. The Municipals were stationed around City Hall while the Metropolitans, in civilian clothes, were posted at the street commissioner's office in the nearby Hall of Records.

At 9AM Conover entered the office clutching his appointment from the governor. The ante room was filled with police from the two departments and friends of the rival commissioners. Conover announced that he was assuming the role of street commissioner and that Mr. Turner would remain in his role as deputy superintendent, and that all the clerks in the office would be retained. Turner said he did not recognize the right of the governor to appoint his successor and therefore could not recognize Conover as street commissioner. The dispute between Conover and Turner drew the attention of Officer Masterson and his Municipals. Masterson addressed Turner and asked what the problem was.

Turner said, "I don't recognize Mr. Conover as street commissioner, and I want your protection in prosecuting my duties."

"My orders are to protect you, sir," Masterson replied, "and I will do so."

"Well," Turner said, "keep your force here and see that no violence is committed."

Conover began moving towards the private office of the street commissioner. The door was locked and guarded by two Municipal policemen. Conover stopped before approaching the door guards and turned toward Turner. "As street commissioner I demand admission to that room. I wish to enter upon my duties."

Turner ignored Conover but instead addressed the officers at the door. "I do not want anyone to enter that room. I don't recognize him as street commissioner."

Officer Masterson approached Conover. "Mr. Conover, I cannot permit you to enter the room."

Conover did not make an attempt to enter the office. Instead, he seated himself at an empty desk in the ante room and remained seated at the desk for the remainder of the day. Mr. Turner and the clerks took their usual positions in the office, and no business was transacted in the office for the rest of the morning.

At 11AM there had been no threat of violence. Suddenly, a squad of Municipal Police marched up to Turner's desk, prompting Turner's supporters to shout, "Hurrah for Mayor Wood. Them's the boys who can knock the hell out of the Albany men."

After a brief conferral with Turner, however, the police squad withdrew without taking any action and quiet was restored again. The only activity for the rest of the day was when Conover had a meal brought in from a nearby restaurant that he ate at his desk.

It was anticipated that if there was going to be trouble, it would commence at the office closing time. Just before 4PM Officer Masterson was reinforced by a squad of Municipals from the Third Ward, and Captain Speight and his squad of Metropolitans took up positions in the office.

At precisely 4PM Mr. Turner said, "Gentlemen, it is now four o'clock and we must close the office; you will all please retire."

The order was unheeded and was repeated by Officer Masterson with the same result. At this point Mr. Conover attempted to assert his authority. "I am in possession of this office by appointment of the governor of the state. I am the street commissioner, and as such I will maintain my position here unless force is used to expel me. If, gentlemen, you want to see my authority, I will show it." Conover removed the governor's appointment from his pocket and displayed it to the officers.

"I don't care about your authority," Turner sneered. He stepped up to Joseph Pollock, one of the clerks and reiterated his command to vacate the office.

Pollock made clear to Turner his allegiance. "I belong here - I'm a clerk in this office and shall remain here until Mr. Conover tells me to leave."

"Mr. Conover has no authority here," Turner said. "Officer, put him out."

Pollock offered no resistance as two Municipals hurried him out of the office. Turner turned his attention to another clerk named Mr. Peckman, who also voiced his allegiance to Conover and refused to leave the office without his order.

Turner was furious. "I am the street commissioner and I discharge you. You are no longer a clerk with this department."

The Municipal officers unceremoniously ejected Peckman. Captain Speight had temporarily left the office to speak with Alderman Owens, but when he attempted to return to the office, his path was blocked by Municipal officers, who informed him to stay back. The captain paid no attention to the order and pushed his way past the officers. He had only progressed a few feet when he was surrounded by Municipal officers who tried hard to eject him. Speight was a large and powerful man and for a time was successful in resisting their efforts. During the melee he was seized around the throat by a tall, long-armed man in a drab coat who seemed determined to choke him.

"Don't hurt him, Mulligan," several men in the crowd called out, at which point the man released his hold. The man wore no uniform and displayed no badge, but it was asserted he was one of Mayor Wood's most recent appointment as a policeman.

By this time Captain Speight had grabbed onto an iron railing and was resisting ejection with all his might. The situation was becoming more intense as some in the crowd cried, "put him down," and "give him the club."

Speight's fingers were pulled from the railing one at a time and he was finally expelled from the office after suffering nothing more than a torn coat, a rumpled collar, and a few scratches on his hand. The Metropolitan Police outside the office immediately surrounded their captain but no further action against Speight was attempted. The Metropolitans formed a line and marched back to their headquarters on White Street.

Meanwhile, Mr. Conover still occupied the desk in the street commissioner's ante room. Captain Bennett had joined the contingent of Municipal Police and he urged Conover to leave the office stating that there could be no exceptions. Captain Bennett and Officer Masterson advanced toward Conover and again urged him to leave. Conover ignored the order and when Bennett gave the order an entire squad of police ejected Conover while he resisted as much as he could. When he was released on the street friends of Conover gathered around and congratulated him on his effort to resist the illegal ejection.

Captain Bennett appeared on the street and offered his hand to Conover, saying that he was sorry his duty forced him to adopt such harsh measures. Conover accepted the hand and said he had no ill feeling toward anyone present. Even though the day had ended with a handshake and no widespread violence, the next day provided the perfect stage for confrontation.

...

At 8:30AM Officer Masterson placed his squad of Municipals in the street commissioner's outer office to prevent access behind the railing. Inside the railing sat Mr. Turner, Captain Bennett, and a deputy sheriff. The police were drawn up in a semi-circle beginning on each side of the private office door and extending around the room. Officer Masterson instructed his men that should Mr. Conover attempt to pass they must politely forbid him, but if he tried to pass, they must put him out with force.

Mr. Conover arrived at the Hall of Records at 9AM completely unescorted and once again attempted to lay claim to the office of street commissioner. Captain Bennett and Officer Masterson refused him entry behind the railing, once again stating that there were no personal feelings involved with their action. When Conover persisted in trying to get past the railing, Masterson grabbed him by the collar and moved him away from the railing.

Conover settled behind a desk on the outside of the railing and was joined there by Pollock and Peckman, the two clerks who had pledged loyalty to him the day before. A builder appeared with a request for an extension of time for removal of sand from his property. The two clerks prepared the necessary paperwork and Conover signed the extension for the builder. No one attempted to stop Conover from conducting business outside the railing and the atmosphere was peaceful – for about twenty minutes. That is when Captain Bennett received a message from Mayor Wood directing the immediate expulsion of Conover from the office.

Conover refused to leave, and the captain directed his men to proceed with the ejection. Conover did not fight, but he did not comply, forcing the police squad to have to almost carry him out of the office. Once outside, friends and sympathizers of Conover encouraged him to take immediate legal action.

By this time several thousand people had gathered in the vicinity of the Hall of Records and many rumors were running rampant through the crowd. Squads of police marched and counter marched in City Hall Park, and it was looking more and more like a bloody collision between Mayor Wood's Municipal Police and the Metropolitan Police was imminent. Still, the area remained quiet. In the meantime, Conover had proceeded directly to Justice Hoffman of the Supreme Court and obtained a warrant for the arrest of Mayor Wood.

The order of arrest of Mayor Wood for inciting a riot was given to Metropolitan Captain George Washington Walling. The captain immediately proceeded to the mayor's office. He entered without opposition and walking up to the mayor, he placed his hand on his shoulder and said, "I arrest you, sir."

Wood looked at Walling with astonishment, and then turned to his policemen and said, "Men, put this man out!"

Captain Walling was forcibly removed from the office. He proceeded to the recorder's office and explained that he was unable to make the arrest. The recorder issued another warrant that ordered all constables and policemen in the city to assist Captain Walling in arresting the mayor. Recorder James Smith also signed a requisition to bring 150 additional Metropolitan Police to the scene. The additional police arrived under the command of Deputy Superintendent Carpenter. This swelled the number of Metropolitans in the area to over two hundred.

A messenger found Coroner Frederick Perry on the street and notified that he was needed at the courthouse on urgent business. Coroner Perry was shocked when a judge handed him a warrant to arrest the mayor. Perry initially balked at this task, but the judge explained that it was the duty of the sheriff to serve a warrant like this, but if no sheriff was available the duty fell on the coroner. Since the sheriff was siding with the mayor, the judge said it was Perry's responsibility as coroner to act. Perry took the warrant to City Hall, but he was denied access to the mayor by the Municipal Police guarding the mayor's office. Perry returned to the court where he was provided a detail of fifty Metropolitan Policemen to return to City Hall and arrest the mayor.

At 3PM City Hall Park was filled with throngs of people. City Hall was filled with Mayor Wood's Municipal Police, fully equipped, who had been summoned from all the districts. Nearly all the captains were present and the doors to the front entrance of City Hall were locked tight. Squads of Municipal Police stood guard at every entrance to the building.

A half hour later there was a terrible commotion as the crowd ran wildly towards Chambers Street shouting, "Here they come! Pitch into the sons of bitches!"

From the vicinity of the Court of Sessions building marched the Metropolitan Police. They each wore on their hats a ribbon with a number and the words "Metropolitan Police." They were closely pressed by the mob who hooted, hollered, and cheered for the mayor. Captain Jacob Seabring was in command of the Metropolitans, and he continued their advance, stopping only when they reached the steps to the rear entrance of City Hall. There, the crowd became aggressive and rushed toward the Metropolitan men but were quickly repelled. With the crowd handled, Captain Seabring ordered his men to ascend the steps where they were met by the Municipal Police under the command of Captain Wines. Wild fighting broke out, much of it being done by civilians who joined the fray on the side of the Municipals. Clubs were freely used and local roughs who had joined the battle pulled sticks from under their coats. Even Alderman Wilson joined the brawl on the side of the Municipals with his official baton in hand.

The Metropolitans fought bravely, but with the numbers against them they were forced to withdraw, but only momentarily. They reformed and again charged up the steps. The fighting was fierce with men crashing down the steps after being clubbed in the head. It looked as if the Metropolitans were going to succeed in breaching the rear entrance when they were set upon from behind by a huge mob of outsiders. When the Metropolitans turned to address the rear attack, the Municipals attacked from the front. It was too much for the overmatched Metropolitans to withstand. They were split into two groups trying to maintain an organized retreat while tending to their wounded.

It was only fifteen minutes earlier that Captain Seabring departed the recorder's office with his squad of fifty Metropolitans. Now, he was back at the same office tending to twenty wounded men and commenting that his men fought bravely but were cut to pieces, and it was a miracle no one was killed.

General Sanford, in command of the 7th Regiment National Guard was marching up Broadway with the regiment in route to Boston. A messenger summoned the general to the recorder's office where Coroner Perry gave a detailed account of the battle that had just occurred when he tried for the second time to serve an arrest warrant on Mayor Wood. The Recorder pled with General Sanford to detour the regiment into the fight, saying it was the only way they could deal with the five hundred Municipals and thousands in the mob. The general departed, and at about 4PM the 7th regiment was in position outside City Hall.

Coroner Perry, accompanied by General Sanford, entered City Hall and served the writ on the Mayor, who, seeing further resistance useless, submitted to arrest, but he never ended up going to trial. Eventually, the Metropolitan Police Act was declared constitutional by the Court of Appeals, forcing Wood to give up his fight against the Metropolitans. By that time, however, the relationship between the Municipals and Metros had become so bad that the Municipals would go into the city jail and release prisoners arrested by the Metropolitans. These actions were a major contributing factor to the Dead Rabbits Riot.

In the meantime, the city had become greatly demoralized. During the fighting between the rival police departments, crime fighting had been neglected. The ability of the Metropolitan Police District to deal with riots and crime in general had been seriously hampered by the forces working against them. Mayor Wood and the opponents of the Metropolitans resorted to every artifice which their ingenuity could devise to hinder the commissioners in the performance of their duty. The members of the old Municipal force were threatened with instant dismissal by Wood if they recognized the orders of the Metropolitan commissioners.

Even after the Court of Appeals put an end to the Municipal Police, a rival police force was established, called the Day and Night Watch, which patrolled the streets and assumed the duties which devolved into the continued efforts of releasing prisoners arrested by the Metropolitan Police. The police station houses, which by law were transferred to the Metropolitan Police, were withheld; writs issued by the courts were resisted and were only served when the police were seconded by men under arms.

Gangs ran freely on the streets free to assert dominance and settle old scores. One of these gangs was the " Dead Rabbits, " residents of the Five Points' district. Their arch-rival was known as the " Atlantic Guard " or "Bowery Boys. " These two gangs, on the fourth of July, came into a conflict on Bayard Street, near the Bowery. Sticks, stones, and knives were freely used on both sides, and men, women and children were wounded in the melee. A small body of policemen, sent to quell the disturbance, was soon repulsed, and several of their number wounded. The rioters erected barricades in the streets, and great fear prevailed throughout the city. The Seventh Regiment was summoned back from Boston, and the city militia was called out. The riot was not quelled until late in the evening. Six men were killed and over a hundred wounded.

The Dead Rabbits Riot aroused the citizens to the danger of having police departments fighting with each other, and intensified the prejudice against the Municipal Police, which was accused of abetting the rioters. Vigorous measures were at once taken to organize the Metropolitan Police and secure its efficiency.

The rear of City Hall as the Municipal and Metropolitan Police attack one another.

Clockwise from top-left: Superintendent Kennedy, The Broadway Squad, Commissioner Acton, Club Exercise, Inspector Carpenter, Inspector Leonard, Escorting the Ladies, Police telegraph, Quelling a riot, Inspector Woilks, Headquarters – Center: Night arrests on their way through the station house to police court.

THE RIVAL POLICE.

OLD POLICEMAN: "Remember the Old Shop, Sir ; business conducted on the usual principles. Always gave satisfaction, I believe."

NEW POLICEMAN: "Anything in our line to-day, Sir? ; an entirely new assortment of goods—handcuffs in every style. Billy's adapted to the meanest capacity ; a young firm, Sir ; only give us a trial."

Simeon Draper – a Metropolitan Police Commissioner

John Warren Nye – A Metropolitan Police Commissioner

CHAPTER 4: PUTTING THE HOUSE IN ORDER

With the Metropolitans established as the one police department for New York City, it was time for the commissioners to tend to the business of running the department. On November 7th, 1857, Pelatiah Perit, of New York, was appointed a commissioner in place of Mr. Draper. Soon after, the Board was enjoined from making further appointments, on the allegation that the dismissal of the old force was illegal. This injunction was dismissed on November 28th, 1857.

The Metropolitan Police station houses were located as follows:

First Precinct, Franklin Market

Second Precinct, No. 49 Beekman Street

Third Precinct, No. 79 Warren Street

Fourth Precinct, No. 9 Oak Street

Fifth Precinct, No. 49 Leonard Street

Sixth Precinct, No. 9 Franklin Street

Seventh Precinct, Gouverneur Market

Eighth Precinct, No. 126 Wooster Street

Ninth Precinct, No. 94 Charles Street

Tenth Precinct, Grand and Ludlow Streets

Eleventh Precinct, Union Market

Twelfth Precinct, 126th Street near Fourth Avenue.

Thirteenth Precinct, Delancey and Attorney Streets

Fourteenth Precinct, No. 53 Spring Street

Fifteenth Precinct, No. 220 Mercer Street

Sixteenth Precinct, No. 156 West Twentieth Street.

Seventeenth Precinct, No. 75 First Avenue.

Eighteenth Precinct, 22nd Street near First Avenue.

Nineteenth Precinct, 59th Street near Second Avenue.

Twentieth Precinct, No. 212 West 35th Street.

Twenty-first Precinct, No. 34 East 29th Street.

Twenty-second Precinct, Corner Eighth Avenue and 48th Street.

Twenty-fourth Precinct, Harbor Police

Twenty-fifth Precinct, Detective force

Twenty-sixth Precinct, force assigned especially for the enforcement of ordinances.

Up to the middle of July 1857 there were not on average more than 500 policemen actually doing duty, whereas, under the Municipal Police, there were upwards of 1,200.

On August 21st. the commissioners authorized the precincts to staff their commands with the correct number of officers and patrolmen. These additional policemen had to be made from the limited number of 860 regular patrolmen, from whom many had to be taken from assignments at the Court of Sessions and Police District Courts, the Commissioners' office, and the General and Deputy Superintendent's offices, and for other contingent and necessary duties. It was clear to see that the police force was inadequate to provide protection to the city. With a population of 820,000, and rapidly increasing, the force numbered but 157 more than when the population was 350,000.

The commissioners drew the attention of the legislature to these facts and argued that the city and its suburbs should be policed by a force adequate to patrol every street and lane by day and by night. Attention was also called to the fact that the beats of the Patrolmen at this time (1858) were in many instances two miles in length, and in several of the precincts, which contained forty thousand inhabitants, there could be detailed for regular duty during the day only eight men.

This was an anxious period for the recently organized Metropolitan Police force. Its trials and troubles were many and grievous. It was the duty of the Common Councils of New York and Brooklyn to furnish suitable stations that were properly heated, but the administrations of the two cities had failed in this responsibility. Many of the station houses were so out of repair as to be unfit for human habitation. Others were so poorly ventilated or so limited in size that they facilitated the spread of disease.

Platoons of twenty men were crowded into small and imperfectly ventilated rooms. The police surgeons designated many of the stations as pest-houses, so fruitful were they of disease. The cellars of the station houses were divided into prisoner cells, and into rooms for the homeless. The stench that arose from these rooms poisoned the atmosphere of the whole building.

In the latter part of 1859, the police commissioners drew up and published a series of rules and regulations for the government and guidance of the force. General Superintendent Pilsbury, in his address to the police, said: "The uniform you wear should be a perpetual coat of mail, to guard you against every temptation to which you may be exposed, by reminding you that no act of misconduct, or breach of discipline, can escape public observation and censure. By exemplary conduct and manly deportment, you will command the respect and cordial support of all good citizens. For the faithful performance of the important trusts committed to your care, you will be noticed approvingly, and your services will be appreciated by the community. And again, every policeman must be circumspect in his deportment, erect and manly in his carriage, and scrupulously discreet in his language and he must be firm, but courteous, in the exercise of his authority. He must be neat and soldierly in his appearance. under any circumstances, use vulgar or profane language. acts."

The general superintendent was by law the executive head of the whole police force of the Metropolitan Police District, and it was the duty of the members of force to respect and obey him accordingly. It was his duty to respond in person to all serious or extensive fires in the cities of New York and Brooklyn. He was also required to respond to all riots or tumultuous assemblages within the district and take command of the police present at the scene, to save and protect property, and arrest such persons as he might find disturbing the peace, or inciting others to do so. The general superintendent had the power to direct, temporarily, any, or all, of the police force, to any place within the district where their services might be deemed necessary. He had the supervision of the public health of the district, and it was his duty to communicate to the Board of Police and to the mayors of New York and Brooklyn the presence of any contagious or infectious disease, or the existence of any nuisance in the district which might be detrimental to the public health.

The returns and reports of commanding officers of any patrol force stationed elsewhere than in the cities of New York and Brooklyn, were made to the general superintendent. It was his duty to see that the laws of the state and the ordinances of the city, town, and village authorities, were duly enforced throughout the district.

Under the direction of the general superintendent, the deputy superintendents had supervision of the police force. It was their duty to see that the orders and directions of the general superintendent in relation to the dress, discipline, deportment, and duties of members of the force were promptly obeyed, and the rules and regulations of the Police Board enforced.

The captains of police were held strictly responsible for the preservation of the public peace in their respective precincts, and to ensure good order, they were vested with the power to post the men under their command in such parts of their precincts, and to assign them such duties, as they might deem expedient. In case of sickness, or the absence of the captain from the police station house, or from his precinct, the duties required of him were performed by one of the sergeants of the precinct, selected for that purpose by the general superintendent. The sergeant so selected, during the absence of the captain possessed and exercised all the powers of a captain and enforced the rules. and regulations established for the government of the precinct.

The prevention of crime should be the most important concern of a patrolman. He should examine and make himself perfectly acquainted with every part of his beat, and vigilantly watch every description of people passing his way and should, to the utmost of his power, prevent the commission of assaults, breaches of the peace, and all other crimes about to be committed, and by his vigilance, render it extremely difficult for anyone to commit crime on his beat. The absence of crime would be considered the best proof of efficiency of the patrolman, and, when on any beat offences frequently occur, there would be good reason to suppose that there was negligence or want of ability on the part of the person in charge of the beat.

Persons appointed to serve on the Metropolitan Police force should:

First: Be able to read and write the English language.

Second: Be citizens of the United States.

Third: Have been residents of the Metropolitan Police District during a term of five years preceding their appointment.

Fourth: Never have been convicted of crime.

Fifth: Be at least five feet eight inches in height.

Sixth: Be not over thirty-five years of age.

Seventh: Be of good health and sound body.

Eighth: Be of good moral character.

Any member of the police force might be immediately dismissed from office, in addition to any other punishment he might be subject to by law, when any of the following charges were substantiated:

First: Intoxication.

Second: Willful disobedience of orders.

Third: Violent, coarse, or insolent language or behavior to a superior, or other person.

Fourth: Receiving money, or other valuable thing, contrary to the Rules and Regulations, or the Statutes of the State.

Fifth: Willful non-compliance with the Rules and Regulations.

Sixth: Inefficiency, or gross neglect of duty.

Seventh: Willfully maltreating or using unnecessary violence toward a prisoner or citizen.

Eighth: Any member of the police force who was found neglecting the payment of his just debts for necessaries or rent, or was found guilty of any act of insubordination or disrespect toward his superior officers, or others, or conduct unworthy of his station, might be reprimanded, fined, or have deductions made from his pay, proportioned to his offense, or, in cases of repeated violations of the rule, might be dismissed.

No person should be terminated from the police force except upon written charges, preferred against him to the Board of Police, and after receiving an opportunity to be heard in his own defense, as prescribed by the law.

The mode of trial, when charges had been preferred, was by taking the testimony on oath against and for the accused officer and reducing the testimony to writing. The written testimony may be taken before one or more of the police commissioners for a decision.

The dress of the general superintendent was a blue dress coat with police buttons.

The dress of the deputy superintendents, captains, and sergeants was a double- breasted frock coat, with police buttons, and blue pantaloons.

Patrolmen on duty, unless specially authorized to appear in citizen's dress, on all occasions wore a black stock, a frock coat of navy blue cloth, single-breasted, and with rolling collar, nine buttons on the breast, two buttons on the hips, also two buttons on the bottom of the skirt; blue waistcoat and blue pantaloons, on the outer seams of which there was a white cord. The coat was buttoned at all times when on duty.

Captains, sergeants, and patrolmen, when on duty, wore caps, shields, badges, emblems, devices, belts and buttons, corresponding to a sample deposited in the office of the general superintendent, and the time of wearing them was directed by him.

Deputy Superintendent Daniel Carpenter, in his quarterly report, ending January 31, 1859, mentioned some of the causes of crime, namely: there were at this date 7,779 places where intoxicating liquors were sold at retail. From the reports of the captains of nineteen precincts it appeared that there were 496 known houses of prostitution. These included 170 lager beer and drinking saloons, combined with houses of ill- fame; 185 low groggeries, where known thieves and fallen women daily and nightly resorted, but a strict police surveillance was kept over them, thereby preventing them from committing depredations that they otherwise would.

The Board of Supervisors had shortly before increased the patrol force to 1,250 men. On November 1st,1859, there were altogether 1,699 persons belonging to the Metropolitan Police Department, namely:

1 General Superintendent

2 Deputy Superintendents,

6 Chief, Deputy and Property Clerks

5 Surgeons

32 Captains

135 Sergeants

1,327 Policemen on patrol duty

118 Policemen on detailed duty

73 Doormen

The sick list in 1859 averaged during the last quarter 46 persons daily. On an average, each patrolman in New York lost 2 1/2 during the quarter by sickness. The aggregate lost time, by reason of sickness and disability, during this quarter, was 365 days.

The Metropolitan Act was amended by the legislature on April 10, 1860. The Metropolitan Police District was then made to comprise the counties of New York, Kings, Westchester and Richmond, and the towns of Newtown, Flushing and Jamaica, in the county of Queens.

The Governor appointed the following as police commissioners: John G. Bergen, Amos Pilsbury, and James Brown. Pilsbury resigned, and Thomas C. Acton was appointed in his place.

On May 23, 1860, the Board appointed John A. Kennedy superintendent of police in place of Amos Pilsbury, who was appointed commissioner before subsequently resigning.

The designation of rank was as follows under the amendment to the Act: superintendent, inspectors, captains, sergeants, patrolmen and doormen. The office of deputy superintendent was abolished.

The following personnel were appointed Inspectors: Daniel Carpenter, John S. Folk, George W. Dilks, and James Leonard.

This Act essentially modified the constitution of the Board of Police, by reducing the number of its members, and by enlarging its powers, and confiding to it new and important duties. By the provisions of the Act of 1857, the Board of Police consisted of five commissioners and the mayors of the cities of New York and Brooklyn. The number of commissioners was reduced to three, and the mayors of New York and Brooklyn were relieved from the police duties which had been imposed upon them. The change was not without its advantages. It secured, for instance, harmony of action, and the constant attention of the members of the Board to the important trusts confided to them.

Besides the principal office in City Hall, up to 1844, there was a police headquarters branch office at the corner of Bowery and Third Street. The office hours were from 9AM until sunset. One of the magistrates received the watch at daybreak every morning, which duty was performed weekly by each magistrate alternately. In 1857, at the time of the conflict between Mayor Wood and the newly appointed police commissioners, the headquarters was moved from City Hall to No. 88 White Street, and six months later to No. 413 Broome Street, and in 1863, to the building at No. 300 Mulberry Street. The Mulberry

Street Headquarters, with the land and buildings, and the additions made in 1868 and 1869, cost $230,860.90.

The area of territory embraced in the Metropolitan Police District was 920 square miles, and the population estimated at 1.4 million persons. Except in the cities of New York and Brooklyn, there was no police force permanently stationed in any part of the district, and in those cities the force was quite inadequate for the population they contained.

In the cities of Europe, where the police were sustained by the constant presence of a military force, there was a policeman to about every 500 inhabitants, while in the city of New York, the proportion was 1 to 650, and in the city of Brooklyn it was 1 to 1,380.

The Embassy from the Government of Japan, which visited the City of New York in June 1860 gave to the Board for the benefit of the Metropolitan Police, the sum of $13,750, with the recommendation that it should constitute a fund, and that the annual interest be distributed among the force in such manner as the Board should deem expedient. The fund was called the Japanese Merit Fund, the interest of which, it was directed, should be distributed in the following manner:

To the Captain who should have best performed his duty for the preceding year - $200.

To the two Sergeants who should have best performed their duty - $125 each.

To the five Patrolmen who should have best performed their duty - $100 each.

The Act of April 24, 1862, provided that constables elected or appointed after the passage of this Act, should be denominated the " Marshals of the City of New York, " and they should have the same power, and perform all the duties that had previously been attached to the office, and each of said marshals should be a resident of the district wherein the court, for or to which he should be appointed, was located. Such marshal should execute a bond, with two sufficient sureties, in the penal sum of $1,000. All laws relating to the election of constables were repealed.

At the request of the Federal authorities, the Board, in the month of July, began to recruit for volunteers to serve in the armies of the United States. To defray the expenses of recruiting, the members of the police and others subscribed the sum of $28,669.15; and by reaching out to the public obtained and additional $77,739.46, which was appropriated to the families of recruits. The Board, with the means thus afforded them, was enabled to place five regiments of infantry and four companies of one hundred men each, of cavalry, in the field.

In 1862, the rule of the department was when sickness or disability resulted from extraordinary exertion or exposure, in discharge of police duty, the full time lost was paid for. When it resulted from ordinary circumstances, one-half the lost time was paid for. When it was feigned, or resulted from carelessness, excess, or fault of the policeman, no pay was allowed for the lost time.

Drilling a Squad of Policemen.

Commissioner Acton

The Eldridge Street Jail.

Parade of the Metropolitan Police in New York City

TO THE

MEMBERS OF THE METROPOLITAN POLICE FORCE.

NEW YORK, *March 4th, 1863.*

Upwards of sixty of your comrades are now in the service of our country, imperiling their lives, sacrificing their health, and undergoing all the hardships and deprivations of a soldier's life, in defending the Constitution and the Government which our Revolutionary Fathers achieved and bequeathed to us, and upholding the national flag—that emblem of liberty and terror to tyrants—from being torn to tatters and trampled under the feet of traitors.

When these brave men resigned from the Department to aid in the holy cause of restoring and preserving the Union, we pledged them our sacred honor that we would keep their families from suffering want so long as they were battling for the nation's life. So far that pledge has been kept, and I have the fullest confidence it will be continued as long as the necessity that called it forth exists. The amount required from each member of the force is the small pittance of fifty cents a month. The good that it accomplishes is beyond calculation. It keeps from forty to fifty families united, and from suffering the pangs of want that, in many instances, they would have suffered, but for this fund. It is well known to you that the pay of the army has been rather uncertain and at long intervals. In some instances Captain Walling and myself felt authorized (by a resolution of the delegates) to aid the families of some who went out as, and now are, officers. In no instance, however, without first being satisfied of the necessity of it,—some of them not having received any money from their husbands for several months, owing, as previously stated, to the army not being paid promptly.

The wives of Sergts. Whitlock and Twaddle and Patrolman Pross, who were killed in battle while at the head of their respective companies, are continued on the pay-roll. Their circumstances are such that, but for the aid they get from the Police Relief Fund, they would have suffered for the necessaries of life the past winter. This, I believe, will be sanctioned by every member of the force.

Annexed will be found a report to me from Mr. Wm. H. Bergen, Clerk to the Treasurer, John G. Bergen, Esq. It is a clear digest of the amount of money collected in the aggregate, and the amount paid out, for the months of December, 1862, and January and February, 1863. I earnestly hope it will be satisfactory to the members of the force, as showing them how beneficially and carefully the money collected from them for the Police Relief Fund has been distributed.

Respectfully,

DANIEL CARPENTER,

President.

Letter Re: the fund to provide money to families of police officers serving in the Union Army.

Dated Oct 1st 1862.

The Board of Police acknowledge, with thanks, the sum of $5 dollars, received from H. H. & Co. to aid families of Recruits in Metropolitan Regiments.

By order of Board of Police.

Peter [Squires], Captain of 2d Precinct.

Receipt acknowledging a donation to the fund.

CHAPTER 5: THE DRAFT RIOT

In July of 1863 the tide of the Civil War had turned against the Confederacy. With no end to the conflict in sight, combined with the fearful loss of life, the Federal Government was finally compelled to resort to a draft to maintain adequate levels of the Union Army. The draft was authorized by an Act of Congress passed in March 1863 and President Lincoln's proclamation, ordering the levy of three hundred thousand men was dated April 8th. It wasn't until July, however, that the draft was scheduled to commence.

At the beginning of July, the Confederate Army had invaded Pennsylvania, prompting New York Governor Seymour to direct General Sanford, commander of the city militia, to send every available regiment at his disposal to Pennsylvania for thirty days' service. While the troops were absent, the United States authorities attempted to enforce the draft in New York City, which caused a terrible insurrection.

The draft met with bitter opposition. There were many people who believed that the use of a draft as a method to raise soldiers was contrary to the spirit of American institutions. But the principal source of discontent lay deeper. It grew out of a hidden sympathy with the Southern cause, which pervaded large classes of persons in the North. If a conscription were enforced these persons saw that they might be obliged to fight in the Union armies against the side with which they sympathized, or, at best, in furtherance of a cause for which they had no love. Thus, it happened that from the very day of the proclamation, symptoms of trouble were discernable.

The process the Federal Government used in carrying out the draft was not very well thought out, especially considering how unpopular it would be in cities like New York. Instead of providing quota numbers and then allowing the individual states to handle the operational aspects of the draft, the War Department sent its provost marshals into the various districts to take direct charge of the selection of the conscripts. This policy increased the popular outrage, and, during the preliminary work, signs and omens of coming trouble were obvious in New York.

In the Ninth Conscription District, which included the lower part of the city, Captain Joel T. Erhardt, the Provost Marshal, narrowly escaped with his life while performing the necessary duty of collecting the names of those liable to be drafted. He was ordered by Colonel Nugent, the Provost Marshal for the whole city, to personally collect the names of some workmen engaged on a building at the corner of Liberty Street and Broadway, who had refused to register when the regular enrolling officers approached them. Captain Erhardt was assailed, in the performance of his duty, by a man armed with an iron crowbar. He drew his pistol and stopped the attack, but after waiting a long time in vain for aid, he was compelled to retreat before an infuriated mob.

More than one incident like this created anxiety among the authorities as the date for the draft drew near, and yet it was doubtful there was actually any organized movement in the city to resist the draft. Information was received by the police of a plan to seize the State Arsenal at Seventh Avenue and 35th Street on Saturday, July 11th, the day on which the drafting was scheduled to begin. It was never revealed whether there was going to be an actual attempt to take the arsenal, but the police presence at the arsenal directed by Superintendent Kennedy assured no attempt would be made.

When the first acts of violence were committed on Monday, the 13th, it was likely that the members of the mob were acting on individual rage with no ideas beyond that of breaking up the draft, and perhaps taking vengeance on some of the officials in charge of it. That afternoon and the succeeding days, an entirely new element entered into the chaos. The thirst for violence had grown furious. The craving to loot and plunder had taken possession of the poorer elements of the population with the draft becoming a mere pretext for lawlessness.

At the outbreak of the violence the police force was under the management of Commissioners Thomas C. Acton and John G. Bergen. The third Commissioner, Bowen, had resigned to accept a brigadier general's commission. John A. Kennedy was Superintendent, and Daniel Carpenter, George W. Dilks and James Leonard were Inspectors.

The drafting began on Saturday, July 11th. There was no special disturbance, but the whole city was uneasy. Sergeant Van Orden, with fifteen men, took possession of the Seventh Avenue Arsenal to foil the previously mentioned plot. A crowd gathered about the building, but the reinforced police presence, prevented any attack from being made.

The drafting took place peacefully and people began to hope that the danger was over, and that the popular discontent would not reach the point of open rioting. Under more favorable circumstances this might have been the outcome, but the day was not so favorable. All the Sunday newspapers came out with long lists of the conscript's names. These were eagerly scanned in all the tenements of the city. People found the names of relatives and friends among the number, and their rage grew in proportion. All day excited groups of unemployed men and women discussed the situation in the houses, in the streets, and, above all, in the liquor saloons, and by midnight they were ready for war – not in Pennsylvania or Virginia, but in the streets of New York City.

Monday's sun rose hot and angry upon the seething city. The people came pouring from the tenement houses to face the fact that the government was once again going to attempt to raid their household to fill a quota for the war. Vainly confident in the strength of their numbers and their passion, they determined that this would not be.

Superintendent Kennedy, though not fully aware of the force of the coming storm, could see that danger was ahead. The drafting was to proceed at two points - No. 1190 Broadway, near 29th Street, and the marshal's office on the corner of Third Avenue and 46th Street.

Superintendent Kennedy began by collecting a force of policemen at headquarters and sending the reserves of the Twentieth Precinct to aid in the defense of the arsenal. The drafting office at No. 1190 Broadway lay within the Twenty- ninth Precinct, and accordingly, Captain Speight took charge of it at 9AM. He brought with him twenty of his own men, and with additional men added from other precincts Speight commanded a total force of 69-policemen, more than enough to handle the crowd outside the arsenal.

The draft proceeded peacefully until noon, when it was adjourned. Captain Speight and his forces remained in the street dispersing various crowds until about 4PM, at which time he was summoned back to headquarters. The mob grew to huge proportions and the excitement was intense. The police were hooted, and curses were shouted not only against the draft, but against African Americans, the National Government, and all public officials. Only a spark was needed to bring about the final explosion. That spark was supplied when someone shouted, "Stop the cars."

An instantaneous rush was made. Horses were uncoupled, drivers were forced from their platforms, and terrified passengers were driven from their places into the depths of the swaying, shouting mass of humanity that filled the Avenue. But now the mob was ready for action. With one awful movement it launched itself upon the band of police defending the marshal's office. The shock was irresistible. One might as well have tried to dam the Hudson River as opposed that mob.

There was a momentary struggle before the police were forced to retreat to the inner area within the building. A hurricane of stones now assailed the windows and doors, which speedily gave way. Then the mob dashed in and joined in hand-to-hand combat with the police. The Marshal and his clerks escaped through the rear of the building. The police slowly followed, fighting all the way, until they emerged onto 46th Street. By this time all the furniture in the office was demolished, and the mob proceeded to set the building on fire. The police attempted to save the property in the adjoining houses but were bitterly assailed at every step. Several policemen were seriously injured in the ensuing combat. Finally, when it became evident that no good could be done while the men were receiving terrible punishment, Captain Porter gave the signal for retreat. The force scattered into small groups, and made their way, as best they could, to several station houses.

At this disastrous moment, purely by chance, Superintendent Kennedy put in an appearance on the scene. Mr. Kennedy's fears of riot had arisen that Monday morning, mainly from the intelligence which reached him shortly after 7AM, that the street contractor's men in the Nineteenth Ward had not gone to work at the usual hour. He at first deemed it sufficient to strengthen the police forces at the marshal's office on Third Avenue, in the manner already detailed, but as the progress of the morning brought fresh indications of trouble, he telegraphed to all the precincts to call in as reserves all the men who had gone off duty at 6AM.

Towards 10AM, with all his arrangements in place, Kennedy took his wagon, and started on a tour of personal inspection. First, he called on Captain Speight, at No. 1190 Broadway, and then visited the arsenal, leaving at each point directions to cover any emergency that might arise. Finally, he turned his horse to the east, and about noon approached the quarter where, unknown to him, the first battle of the riot had been fought. The Superintendent was not in uniform and was totally unarmed. In what could be debated as being either courageous or stupid Kennedy left his wagon and walked through the angry crowd towards a fire the mob had ignited.

Everything seemed very quiet, until, suddenly, someone cried out, "There's Kennedy!"

"Where, where?"

"Where is he?" demanded a thousand angry voices.

He was pointed out, and before he had time to realize the situation, a blow from behind sent him down an embankment six feet high into a vacant lot. In an instant the superintendent was on his feet running for his life across the lots, while the infuriated mob chased him. He was able to outrun his pursuers and succeeded in climbing the 47th Street embankment. But here a fresh crowd, as brutal as the first, was waiting for him. They came at him with a rush, and for the second time he was hurled to the foot of the embankment. Kennedy regained his feet, but the crowd continued to follow him. A burly ruffian tried to dash his brains out with a club, and Kennedy with difficulty protected his head. By this time, he must have received fully fifty blows on various parts of his body. He now turned and ran toward Lexington Avenue, where there was a pond or mud hole of considerable width and depth.

"Drown him, drown him!" shouted the rioters, and a tremendous blow sent Kennedy into the pond, where his face struck on some stones at the bottom and was frightfully lacerated. But he was able to maintain consciousness. Making his way through the mud and water through which his pursuers were unwilling to follow, he reached Lexington Avenue before they got around.

As he emerged from the pond he met Mr. John Eagan, a prominent citizen, and begged for aid. Mr. Eagan possessed sufficient influence with the mob to prevent them from doing any further violence, and Kennedy, now fainting with pain and exhaustion, was laid on a common feed wagon and driven to headquarters. As the wagon drove up to the building, Commissioner Acton was standing on the steps. He noticed the bruised and bleeding man, but never guessed who it was, so far beyond recognition was the superintendent. When he realized it was Kennedy, he had him transported to the house of a friend, and surgical aid was procured. It was found that no bones were broken, and unbelievably, the superintendent returned to duty on the Thursday following, a fact all the more amazing considering he was over sixty years of age.

The early disablement of the superintendent placed the command of the force upon the shoulders of Commissioner Acton, at headquarters, and of Inspector Daniel Carpenter in the field—or rather in the streets. Both proved equal to the demands upon them. To no one man was the speedy suppression of the riots due so largely as to Mr. Acton. His very first step showed his consummate generalship. The moment he realized the extent of the disorder, on seeing Superintendent Kennedy's terrible condition, he telegraphed to every precinct, except the Twelfth, from which the rioters had cut off communication, ordering the entire force to concentrate at the Central Office. He also dispatched the Steamboat Squad with their vessel, under Captain Todd, to transport to the city all the Federal troops that could be spared from the forts in the harbor, and subsequently to land arms for volunteer troops. Acton did not leave the Central Office for five days, except for a couple of short periods on official business. From 6AM on Monday morning until after 2AM the following Friday, he never closed an eye in sleep. An able assistant to Acton during the riot was Commissioner John G. Bergen who was constantly at headquarters for hours almost equal to Acton and sharing in all his labors. Chief Clerk Seth C. Hawley was also a most valuable aid. He was placed in charge of the ordinance department, serving out the arms and ammunition needed by the men as they started on their repeated expeditions. He also provided for the wants of the wounded and did all in his power to furnish accommodations for the crowds of refugees who early began to flock to headquarters. He had also to provide sustenance to the police, military, and refugees, in all over five thousand persons, for an entire week.

About the time Superintendent Kennedy was being beaten, another fierce scene was in progress only a few blocks away. When messages of Captain Porter's desperate situation at the marshal's office were transmitted, several contingents from various precincts were dispatched to Captain Porter's aid, not realizing that Porter and his men had already made their escape from the location. Among the first of these intended reinforcements to arrive on the scene was a squad of thirteen men from the Eighth Precinct, under Sergeant Ellison. This squad first encountered the mob at Third Avenue and 44th Street. A desperate hand-to-hand fight ensued. The mob fought furiously, and the police were outnumbered a hundred to one, and were soon forced to retreat. Sergeant Ellison, who had been terribly beaten, remained a prisoner in the rioter's hands. At that moment, Sergeant Wade arrived with his squad from Broadway and the fight was renewed, and Ellison was extricated from his captivity more dead than alive. He had defended himself bravely with his revolver and a gun which he had wrested from a rioter. but he had been overwhelmed by numbers, terribly beaten, and pelted with stones until he lost consciousness. After lying as if dead for half an hour on the pavement, he was carried by two of his comrades to the Twenty-first Precinct station house. In this fight, too, Officer Van Buren had his leg broken, and many other officers were seriously injured.

A platoon from the Ninth Precinct arrived at 44th Street and Third Avenue at the same time as Sergeant Wade, and joined the fight, but they were still badly outnumbered. Just as the police were facing imminent defeat, Sergeant McCredie, of the Fifteenth Precinct arrived at 43rd Street and Third Avenue with fourteen men. He was joined by ten men from the Twenty-eighth, under Sergeant Wolfe, and by the scattered men from the other precincts, until his force numbered forty-four. With this force, small as it was, McCredie-who was deservedly christened by his comrades "Fighting Mac" began a furious onslaught on the mob that filled the avenue. He met with a stubborn resistance, but his men were able to force their way to 46th Street, where they hoped Captain Porter and his men still held their ground. When they found Porter and his men were gone, McCredie and his men found themselves hemmed in on all sides by masses of infuriated men. Stones rained in on them. Nine of the fourteen men from the Fifteenth Precinct were badly wounded before they were able to disperse the mob.

Officer Bennett was knocked down three times before he was knocked unconscious. In that condition, he was stripped to his drawers, and savagely beaten. At last, his seemingly dead body was taken by strangers to St. Luke's Hospital and brought the hospital deadhouse (mortuary). His grief- stricken wife was brought to the hospital to claim the remains of her deceased husband. Her grief changed to astonishment when it was discovered that her husband's heart was still beating. Doctors immediately went to work, and Bennett recovered, although his recovery period was very long and arduous.

Officer Travis, also of the fifteenth precinct, was also taken to St. Luke's. In trying to escape the crowd he was confronted by a man with a pistol. He captured the weapon, but before he could use it, was knocked down and beaten almost to a jelly. His jaw and right hand were broken. The mob stripped him naked before they left him.

Sergeant McCredie was disabled by a blow on the wrist from a bar of iron. His life was saved by a young German woman, who hid him between two mattresses while the rioters searched her house from roof to cellar.

There were many other policemen badly beaten, and this was not the only collisions between bodies of police and the rioters. A force had been ordered to the scene from the Eighteenth Precinct with Sergeant Vosburgh in command. It was unable to affect a junction with Captain Porter, and after a brief, but courageous struggle, was forced to retreat. There were at least three other attempts from various precincts to rescue Captain Porter and his men, who were no longer in need of a rescue.

With the success the mob achieved against the police response, they dispersed throughout the city, looting and burning in all directions, and attacking African Americans whenever encountered. Some of the more level-headed rioters realized that for any lasting success, arms would be absolutely necessary. At about 1:30PM a portion of the mob gathered outside the large gun factory at 21st Street and Second Avenue, where a great quantity of firearms were known to be in storage. This movement had been anticipated, and early in the afternoon, Sergeant Banfield, with a squad from the Eighteenth Precinct took possession of the building. Later, they were relieved by the Broadway Squad of 32-men under Sergeant Burdick and Roundsmen Ferris and Sherwood. The men reached the factory singly or in pairs, escaping the notice of the rioters, who, as 3PM approached, had swelled to thousands in number. Every policeman was armed with a carbine and stationed at a window. Finally, the battle began.

A whirlwind of stones, bricks and bullets was launched against the doors and windows. The defenders did not show themselves and the fire of the mob was not returned. An effort was initiated to burn the building, but it failed, and the attack was renewed with greater fury than ever.

One of the rioters attacked the building door with a sledgehammer. A crowd of rioters gathered around the door until at last, a blow from the hammer resulted in a panel on the door crashing in. The man stooped to crawl into the opening when the single shot of a carbine was heard, and the man fell back with a bullet through his skull. The rioters hesitated, but only for a moment. The attack was quickly renewed, and Sergeant Burdick sent a message to Captain Cameron for aid. When the sergeant received word from the captain that no aid was available, Burdick sent a new message indicating that he would not be able to hold the factory. The response from Captain Cameron was to direct Sergeant Burdick to get his men out of the building.

These messages had been carried by Sergeant Buckman, of the Eighteenth Precinct, in disguise, and at great risk. The mob had now been held in check almost four hours, but further resistance was impossible. The only means of retreat, however, which was not cut off, was through a hole in the rear wall of the building, twelve by eighteen inches in size. Through this small hole the policemen squeezed their way, gaining the street through a stone yard. All the police had just cleared the factory when the rioters gained access to it. Shortly thereafter they had to escape from the Eighteenth Precinct station house in plain clothes. They traveled to the Central Office where they performed guard duty all Monday night.

The momentum in the fight to this point had been completely with the rioters, who had achieved victories over the police at every engagement. A change in fortune, however, would soon commence. Moving forward, the police, aided by the military, inflicted a series of crushing defeats on the mob. The first of these was inflicted by a force of two hundred men, under Inspector Daniel Carpenter, at the corner of Broadway and Amity Street. The telegrams sent to all the precincts ordering the concentration of the entire police force at headquarters, by 3PM, caused a considerable number of men to muster there.

Telegrams were now pouring in announcing deeds of destruction in every quarter of the city. Buildings on Broadway and Lexington Avenue were being sacked and burned; police stations were under siege, and, despite the efforts of Fire Chief Decker and his men, the Colored Orphan Asylum, on Fifth Avenue, was wrecked and burned, the young residents narrowly escaping with their lives. The asylum housed two hundred children, besides the officers and matrons. The main building was four stories, with wings of three stories. Superintendent William E. Davis hurriedly fastened the doors, and, while the mob was breaking them in, the children were collected and taken from the building by the rear door before the mob had battered down the barricaded doors. The building was first ransacked and looted. Everything portable was carried away and then the building was set on fire. In a little time, the asylum was wrapped in flames, and within an hour or so only a small portion of the walls remained standing. After their escape from the building the children were taken to the Twentieth Precinct, where they were taken care of by Captain Walling, and were subsequently removed to Blackwell's Island.

Towards four o'clock it was announced that a vast crowd was coming down Broadway to attack police headquarters. This was the moment for action. Drill Officer T. S. Copeland, from the available forces, quickly organized a band of two hundred men, which he himself joined as second in command to Inspector Carpenter.

Carpenter made brief speech. "We are going to put down a mob," he said. "take no prisoners but strike quick and hard."

Then the force marched up Broadway. The rioters were met near Amity Street. They carried an American flag, and a standard of planks with the words "No Draft." They were armed with clubs, pitchforks, crowbars, swords, guns, and pistols. For a minute the opposing bodies stood but a few feet apart.

"By the right flank, company front, double quick, charge!" shouted Carpenter, and in a moment he and his men were upon the mob.

Carpenter drew first blood, fracturing the skull of a ringleader. His men obeyed his orders literally, striking quick and hard on all sides. The crowd wavered, broke, and quickly fled, leaving their banners in the hands of the police, with the pavement strewn with their wounded and dying comrades. The police marched on to Mayor Opdyke's house on Fifth Avenue, which had been threatened, but finding all quiet, marched back to headquarters. The Amity Street battle decided the fortunes of the city. After it, the defeat of the rioters was only a question of time and hard fighting. It was demonstrated that they could not stand up before regular discipline.

Inspector Carpenter, after the Amity Street battle, took a very short rest. Shortly before 8PM Sergeant Copeland organized another battalion of two hundred men, including one hundred men from the Brooklyn Police, who were a part of the Metropolitan Police District, under the command of Inspector John S. Folk. With this force,

Inspector Carpenter started to the Tribune building, which had been threatened all day and had finally been attacked by the rioters, whose wrath was especially venomous against the Tribune's publisher, Horace Greeley, as an abolitionist and advocate of the Union cause.

Before Carpenter and his force could reach the Tribune, he was informed that the building was being sacked. The police approached the scene on the run and reached it simultaneously with a platoon under Captain Bryan from the Fourth Precinct. Sergeant Snodgrass of the Second Precinct had also, by mingling in the crowd, learned of the premeditated attack in time to join the other police squads with the reserve of the Second Precinct. The several squads of police charged the rioters together from different points. Captain Thorne, of the Twenty-sixth Precinct, was knocked down with the blow of a club. Officer Cowen brought his club down on the skull of the man who struck the blow. The rioters fell stunned and bleeding on all sides. Many police officers were also injured.

The mob took flight in all directions. The portion that rushed up Centre and Chatham Streets was pursued by the officers who had dispersed it and were subjected to the maximum use of physical force by the police. The largest section of the mob fled across the open space in front of City Hall, but just at that moment, Inspector Carpenter, with his two hundred men, were wheeling into the same location. Grasping the situation at a glance, the Inspector formed his men in company formation and charged the fleeing mob, inflicting serious physical punishment on the rioters as they fled in all directions. With the situation under control, Inspector Carpenter established a headquarters at City Hall.

No sooner had Inspector Carpenter secured the area around City Hall, than his force was weakened considerably when Inspector Folk and his contingent returned to Brooklyn. Carpenter and his men, however, still had their hands full. A report came in that the houses of

African Americans were being burned in the Sixth Precinct, and that an African American was hanged, and his body burned.

Captain John Jourdan was sent with his men to suppress this disturbance. He had been fighting the rioters all day, and with Sergeants Walsh and McGiven, he dispersed a mob on Baxter Street.

At 6 PM six hundred rioters, who attacked a house at Baxter and Leonard Streets where twenty African American families resided, were dispersed by Captain Jourdan and his men. The fighting was very bitter, and even on their way back to headquarters Jourdan and his men were forced to fight off another mob that assaulted them.

Captain Jourdan returned to City Hall in time to participate in Inspector Carpenter's tour of the Fourth Ward, in the course of which he suppressed four riotous crowds who were burning African American dwellings. Fifty men were left to protect the Tribune building with the remainder of the force accompanying the Inspector.

After this effective tour of the Fourth Ward, Carpenter and his men had one more exploit to perform that busy Monday. At 11PM word was received that a new and great mob was marching down Broadway to raid the Tribune office. Carpenter at once massed his men close to the east gate of City Hall Park, facing three companies to the west, from where the rioters were expected to come, and the balance to the east. The police were concealed by the darkness, and the rioters were allowed to approach within a hundred yards, before Carpenter gave the word "Up Guards, and at them!"

The Police went in with a rush. They were outnumbered by the rioters five to one, but the shock was irresistible, and in a few minutes the park was for the second time strewn with wounded men, while a confused remnant of rioters fled up Broadway. At midnight Carpenter and his fatigued men were relieved by the arrival of Inspector James Leonard with three hundred and fifty men.

Inspector Leonard remained in charge at City Hall until the following Friday, when the riots ended. Leonard's tactics and judgement contributed greatly to the suppression of the rioting in the downtown districts of the city.

At City Hall the Inspector's resources were taxed to the utmost. Before daybreak on Tuesday, he sent a platoon to protect the residences of African Americans at Leonard and York Streets. He orchestrated the dispersal of a mob which was sacking a provision store on Greenwich Street near Cortlandt. He sent a squad to protect Brooks Brothers' clothing store on Catharine Street, and other squads to protect the hotels on Fulton and Cortlandt Streets. Towards morning Carpenter learned that a mob was proceeding to Fulton Ferry to oppose the landing of marines at the Brooklyn Navy Yard, and to burn Fulton Market. He sent a large force of police to meet this mob with the result being a short, sharp fight, ending in the rout of the rioters. Leonard dispatched so many men to different areas that by 9AM he was left alone at City Hall. He went to headquarters at once to state in person that a strong force was required at Printing House Square. He was given two hundred men, and when he hurried back with them, he found an excited crowd rapidly growing in numbers.

Every African American was chased and beaten. By noon, Leonard and a hundred men were able to clear City Hall Park and Printing House Square, much of the police success coming from the liberal use of their clubs. This process had to be repeated a number of times, but by far the most exciting event of the day in this vicinity occurred at 8PM, when a mob beset a company of regular troops at Broadway and Chambers Street and attempted to prevent the soldiers from proceeding. Seeing that an attack was imminent, Inspector Leonard, accompanied only by Sergeant Polly of the Eleventh Precinct, and one patrolman, forced his way into the heart of the crowd, and, in order to direct attention away from the soldiers, seized two of the leaders of the mob and began dragging them towards City Hall. The officers succeeded in focusing the mob away from the soldiers, but they nearly forfeited their lives. The rioters turned their full fury against the three officers, who, each holding on to a rioter, faced the enemy with uplifted clubs.

Shouts of "Kill them - give them what Kennedy got!" filled the air, but, thankfully, the officers' determination allowed them to keep moving through the crowd. As they moved, the officers held their prisoners in front of them, causing the prisoners to receive many cuts and bruises from the missiles aimed by their friends at the police.

Finally, word of the fight reached the police at the City Hall headquarters. Seventy-five men instantly turned out to rescue their comrades. In a few seconds the rescue force had reached the three officers, who then released their battered prisoners into the crowd.

Inspector Carpenter led a charge on the mob which sent it fleeing in all directions, while heaps of injured men marked the track along which the police had moved. This defeat seemed to drain the energy from the riot in that part of the city.

...

The next day some slight encounters took place, but Inspector Leonard faced no more pitched battles. He remained on duty at City Hall until Friday, at which time he and his officers were recalled. In other parts of the city, however, there was still plenty of action. At 2AM Drill Officer Copeland, with a hundred men of the Fourth, Ninth, Nineteenth, Twenty-third, and Twenty- eighth Precincts, marched from headquarters to recover the body of William Jones, an African American whom the mob beat terribly and hanged from a lamppost on Clarkson Street. The mob lit a fire under the body and held it there burning until Copeland and his men dispersed them and took the corpse to Headquarters. On their way back the members of the Twenty-third Precinct received intelligence that their station house, on East 87th Street, as well as numerous private houses in the vicinity, was pillaged and burned by rioters. Doorman Ebling saved the telegraph instrument, but all other property, public and personal, was lost.

At 6AM Inspector Carpenter had moved uptown with two hundred and fifty men, to suppress disorder along Second Avenue. He and his force entered the avenue at 21st Street, and found it crowded with people who hissed and cursed the police but did not stop them from passing through. Then the police reached the point on the avenue between 32nd and 33rd Streets. Here a sudden shower of bricks, paving stones, and bullets, from the windows of the houses, brought the police columns to a halt. Many of the men were hurt, a few were stunned. Inspector Carpenter instantly ordered his men to attack the houses, and to go through them from cellar to roof, and render every rioter who might be encountered incapable of further mischief. The police moved with ruthless aggression. Barricaded doors were smashed in as they commenced their attack with irresistible fury. Some rioters fled to the roofs, only to be overtaken and beaten by the officers. Some of the mob leaped from upper windows and fell shockingly maimed on the street below. Men were hurled downstairs, and others were clubbed into insensibility. The few who made it to the street unhurt fell into the hands of the reserve which Carpenter posted there, and they fared no better than their fellow rioters.

Captain Speight, of the Twenty-ninth Precinct, with his command, had been in the rear of the battalion as it marched up Second Avenue, and sustained the brunt of an attack from the rear. The officers instantly faced about, and Captain Speight led the charge on the mob, but he was brought to the ground by the blow of a brick. He sprang to his feet, and still shouted encouragement to his men. When the crowd was driven off, the men joined in the attack on the houses at the front of the police column.

For a time, the mob had been overmatched by the police attacks, but after the police had marched off, an attack was begun on the soldiers, who fired a volley in reply. Several people, including a woman, were wounded, and the crowd became panic-stricken and scattered.

An hour or two later, Colonel O'Brien, who was in command of the soldiers who had fired on the mob returned to the spot alone. He was recognized, and set upon by the rioters, thirsting for vengeance. The rioters showed no mercy, and the unrecognizable remains of the colonel were recovered after nightfall.

When he had defeated the rioters at 33rd Street, Inspector Carpenter continued his march. He patrolled all the disturbed districts in the uptown. portions of the east side of the city, only returning to Headquarters at 1PM.

At 10AM, Inspector Dilks and a force of two hundred men marched to the protection of a wire factory on Second Avenue and 21st Street, where four thousand carbines were stored. When the Inspector's force arrived, they found the building to be in the possession of the rioters, thousands of whom were congregated on the avenue. The firearms were being passed out of the building by the members of the mob who had entered. The crowd hailed the approaching police with yells of defiance. Although the odds were against him, Dilks did not hesitate a moment. He led his men in a charge on the mob. This was one of the bitterest fights during the entire riot. The mob put up a stubborn resistance, but finally, the discipline of the police prevailed. The immense mob wavered, fled and dispersed. Then the police attacked the factory, an operation that was a repeat of the attack on the houses on 34th Street. The building was recaptured foot by foot, and the punishment inflicted on the rioters was fearful. When the fighting was over, the police gathered up all the firearms they could find and marched with them to headquarters.

The Police had hardly left the neighborhood of the factory when the crowd re-assembled. The building was once more invaded, and a quantity of arms that had escaped the notice of Inspector Dilks' party was discovered. But before the rioters had time to affect a distribution of the weapons, a fresh force of police assailed them. Capt. John C. Helme, of the Twenty- seventh Precinct, had been sent out from

Headquarters with his own men and details from other precincts, to disperse a crowd that was besieging Mayor Opdyke's house on Fifth Avenue. That task was speedily accomplished, and some piles of building material, which might serve as ammunition for the rioters, was removed to places of safety. When Captain Helme heard of the trouble at the wire factory, he marched his men to the location, arriving just as the mob re-assembled after Inspector Dilks' departure-and had for the second time spread through the building. The Police approached from 21st Street and did not wait for any negotiations. Instead, they rushed the mob as they wheeled onto the Avenue. For the second time the rioters fought stubbornly but were driven back after a short struggle. Fifty of the rioters remained disabled on the pavement.

Captain Helme's battalion started for Headquarters, carrying with them the remaining firearms they had recovered from the factory. By this time the mob was reinforced by those who had engaged in the killing of Colonel O'Brien, and, with renewed confidence, it crowded around the police, whose position became very tenuous. The police were in trouble, but Inspector Dilks arrived in the nick of time with a force of two hundred fresh men. The fight which followed was very short. The mob had already received two fearful lessons, and hardly waited for a third. The united forces of Inspector Dilks and Captain Helme now made a tour of the neighborhood, engaging in several sharp fights, in which they were aided by the military. The battalion turned down 22nd Street towards First Avenue, when a galling fire was opened on them from windows and roofs. The soldiers were sent to the front, and, by a well- directed fire, they soon cleared away the riotous sharpshooters.

As the Police wheeled into First Avenue they were confronted by a body of rioters, who rained missiles upon them. The military again advanced and silenced the rabble with several sharp volleys. The rioters retreated slowly, however, and several more volleys were fired at them as the troops and police advanced. At 21st Street the mob broke and fled.

After the police force had withdrawn the mob re-assembled and headed for the Eighteenth Precinct station house on East 22nd Street. The precinct was in the charge of Sergeant Burden and three men. Defending the building was out of the question, so the building was barricaded, and the officers retreated through a rear window. The rioters speedily broke in and burned the building.

Captain Walling was sent with a large force into his own precinct, the Twentieth, where the rioters were making some headway, having beaten a body of soldiers and taken away their guns at Allerton's Hotel, Eleventh Avenue, between 40th and 41st Streets. When he arrived in the neighborhood, the captain learned that marauders were sacking the private residences on 47th Street. He ran with his men to the location just as a group of rioters had broken into Dr. Ward's house and were departing with stolen property from the house and other houses. As the police appeared the thieves fled. The police chased small groups of thieves and recovered most of the property. The only purpose of this mob had been robbery, and this whole section of the city was terrorized by similar bands.

The Police next rushed to the station house on 35th Street, where they telegraphed the military for aid in overcoming a new movement of the rioters, who had cut down the telegraph poles all along Ninth Avenue, from 32nd to 43rd Streets, and with these, and carts, and wagons, bound together with the telegraph wire, had formed barricades across the avenue at 37th and 43rd, and across all the intervening streets. They had also set fire to and burned down the Weehawken Ferry House.

At 6PM Captain Wesson, with a force of regulars, joined the police at the station house, and both bodies moved on the barricades. Captain Slott, of the Twenty-second Precinct, advanced with a body of police to remove the barrier at 37th Street. They were driven off by a volley of stones and bullets. The military advanced, and with a steady fusillade, cleared away the rioters. Then the police returned and removed the barricades. The mob rallied and attacked them a second time but were again beaten off by the fire of the troops. The police then advanced again, and, one by one, all the barricades were demolished.

At midnight there was a new alarm. A great crowd gathered on 30th Street, between Seventh and Eighth Avenues, vowing the destruction of the African American church there. Captain Walling hastened to the spot with his entire force. They charged on the mob unexpectedly but were received with a shower of bullets from the alleys and doorways on either side. The fire was returned and then the officers rushed in, making maximum use of their clubs, so that in a few minutes only prostrate rioters were to be seen. This practically ended the riot in this quarter of the city, but there were still isolated pockets of violence.

Sergeant Devoursney and Officer Gardner, of the Twenty- sixth Precinct, had been stoned while acting as scouts, but had learned of an attack on a house, and reported the news to Captain Bogart. The police returned on the run, and the crowd in the street ran at the sight of the police. The house was full of rioters and robbers, and several officers entered to drive them out, while the main body remained outside to give them a warm reception. As they mob came rushing to the street, Sergeant Burdick of the Broadway Squad felled to the ground a gigantic fellow laden with stolen property. As he did so, a score of bullets whistled through the air, two of which struck the rioter, while one entered Officer Dipple's thigh, and breaking the bone passed up through the marrow, causing inflammation, from which the officer died in a few days.

The reason for the shooting was that the military had arrived suddenly on the scene and noticing the rush of the rioters from the house, had fired wildly, and without orders, doing more injury to the police than to the mob. Officer Hodgson received in this volley of fire a wound to his arm. Officer Robinson was wounded in the thigh. A rioter, as he rushed out, was caught and clubbed by Officer Hill of the Twenty- sixth Precinct. He drew a pistol and shot the officer in the thigh. The next moment he fell riddled with soldiers' bullets. Officer Rice, of the Twenty- sixth, was shot in the groin and thigh. A bullet passed through Sergeant Pell's sleeve. Officer Hanifer had a desperate combat with an immense rioter, whom he drove to the street. During the entire battle the women gave more trouble than the men. Many of them were in the house plundering, and it took the use of police clubs to the fleshiest portions of their persons to make many of them relinquish their ill-gotten treasures.

Tuesday night concluded with another bloody battle, waged downtown near Brooks Brothers' clothing store on Catharine Street. The store had been entered and was being pillaged. The police charged and the mob gave way, many being badly beaten. The officers entered the store, and after fierce combat from floor to floor, cleared it, beating severely some hundreds of the rioters. In the fight, Sergeant Finney, of the Third Precinct, was shot in the face. Sergeant Delaney had his hat knocked off by the wadding of a pistol fired at him by a rioter only a few feet away. While the fight was still in progress, Inspector Carpenter arrived with a detachment from headquarters. He rushed upon the rioters with his men and contributed in no small measure to their punishment. A guard was kept in Brooks' all night.

After this night quiet reigned in the neighborhood. After the dispersion of the mob on Tuesday night, Inspector Carpenter and his command made a tour of the downtown districts, meeting and scattering parties of rioters at several points.

The police mission shifted from battling the mob for possession of the streets to recovery of stolen property. For example, on Friday, Sergeant Brackett, Sergeant Hastings, and thirty-five men, visited the block bounded by First and Second Avenues, 39th and 40th Streets with the Seventh Regiment providing an escort. The area was then one of the worst in the city. Every corner of every shanty was searched, and quantities of stolen goods recovered. Sergeant Vaughan and Roundsman Moore, with small parties, discovered quantities of goods in other parts of the precinct.

During the riot week all the station houses were left inadequately guarded, and great courage and judgment were shown by the police in their preservation. On Sunday, July 18th, a large body of police under Captain Dickson, of the Twenty-eighth Precinct, started for a tour of the small towns along the Hudson River. They were accompanied by a body of troops, and remained away three days, completely squashing all tendencies to revolt that might have existed among the rural population. The day after their return they made similar visits to Staten Island and Flushing.

During the week following the riot the Board of Police Commissioners issued an address to the force, which contained the following:

"Of the inspectors, captains, and sergeants of police who led parties in the fearful contest, we are proud to say that none faltered or failed. Each was equal to the hour and the emergency. Not one failed to overcome the danger, however imminent, or to defeat the enemy, however numerous. Special commendation is due to Drill Sergeant Copeland for his most valuable aid in commanding the movements of larger detachments of the Police. The patrolmen who were on duty fought through the numerous and fierce conflicts with the steady courage of veteran soldiers, and have won, as they deserve, the highest commendations from the public and from this Board. In their ranks there was neither faltering nor struggling. Devotion to duty and courage in the performance of it were universal. The public and the department owe a debt of gratitude to the citizens who voluntarily became special patrolmen, some three-thousand of whom, for several days and nights, did regular patrolmen's duty with great effect. In the name of the public, and of the department in which they were volunteers, we thank them. Mr. Crowley, the Superintendent of the

Police Telegraph, and the attaches of his department, by untiring and sleepless vigilance in transmitting information by telegraph unceasingly through more than ten days and nights, have more than sustained the high reputation they have always possessed. Through all these bloody contests, through all the wearing fatigue and wasting labor, you have demeaned yourselves like worthy members of the Metropolitan Police. The public judgment will commend and reward you. A kind providence has permitted you to escape with less casualties than could have been expected. It is hoped that the severe but just chastisement which has been inflicted upon those guilty of riot, pillage, arson and murder will deter further attempts of that character. Sergeant Young, of the Detective force, aided by Mr. Newcomb and other special patrolmen, rendered most effective service in arranging the commissary supplies for the large numbers of police, military, special patrolmen, and destitute colored refugees, whose subsistence was thrown unexpectedly on the department. The duty was arduous and responsible and was performed with vigor and fidelity. All the clerks of the department, each in his sphere, performed a manly share of the heavy duties growing out of these extraordinary circumstances."

A week of terror and dismay, a week of horrors unparalleled in the history of New York, was drawing to a close. A great city was for a time in the grasp of robbers and cut-throats, and the very existence of the Republic imperiled. But the battle had been valiantly waged and won. The police had saved New York City. Had the rioters succeeded in overpowering the police and military, and gained possession of the city but for one hour, there is no calculating what irreparable calamities might have befallen the city and the Nation.

Process of Drafting in the Sixth District.

Rioters Marching Down Second Avenue.

SACKING A DRUG STORE IN SECOND AVENUE.

FIGHT BETWEEN RIOTERS AND MILITARY.

NEW YORK—THE RIOT IN LEXINGTON AVENUE.

RUINS OF THE PROVOST-MARSHAL'S OFFICE.

Colored Orphan Asylum.

HANGING A NEGRO IN CLARKSON STREET.

Escaping Rioters Surprised by the Police.

Nursing Wounded Policeman.

Brutal Murder of Col. O'Brien.

SCENE AT THE FIVE POINTS RIOT. WOMEN AND MEN THROWING BRICKBATS DOWN ON THE POLICE.

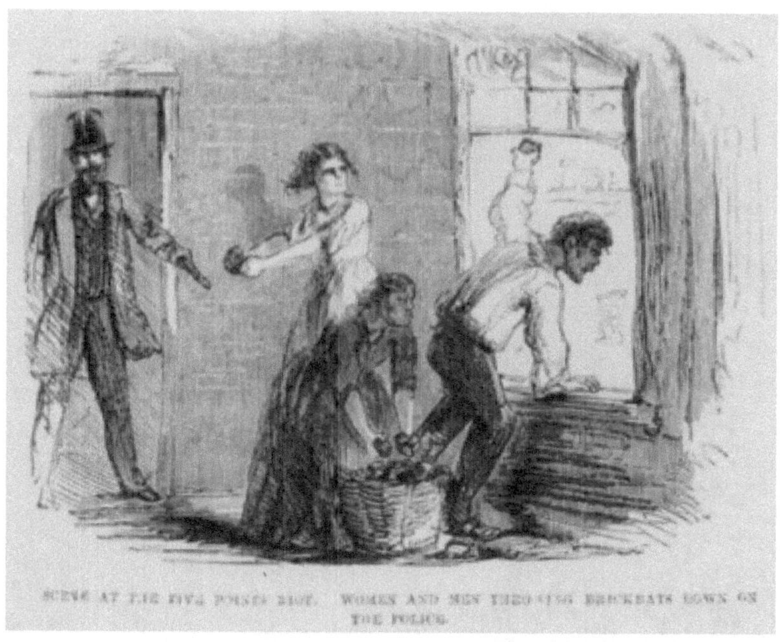

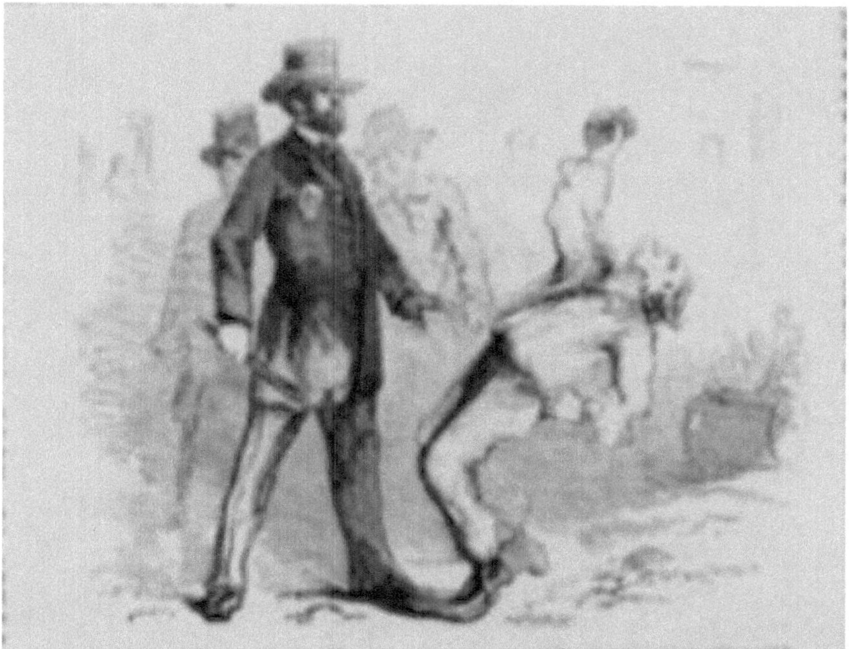

Death of a "Dead Rabbit"

John A Kennedy

Daniel Carpenter

Inspector Speight.

A "Dead Rabbits" barricade on Bayard Street.

CHAPTER 6: BACK TO BUSINESS

At the end of 1863 Commissioner Bowen resigned from the Police Board to accept a commission as a general in the Union Army. On December 31, 1863, Governor Seymour, in a highly politicized move in order to place the Police Board firmly in the control of the Democrats, appointed as police commissioners, Joseph S. Bosworth, William McMurray, and William B. Lewis, in the place of Bergen, Acton and Bowen. Acton and Bergen, however, refused to recognize the governor's power to remove, and remained in sole charge of the police. During the ensuing winter the legislature overruled the governor and passed a law appointing Thomas C. Acton, Joseph G. Bosworth, John G. Bergen, and William McMurray commissioners for periods fixed in the law.

This arrangement was the result of a compromise between the two parties. Acton and Bergan were Republicans and Bosworth and McMurray Democrats, and it was the intent for the equalization of the parties to be maintained in the board. But when the term of McMurray expired in 1866 the legislature elected Benjamin F. Manierre as his successor, thus making the board three Republicans and one Democrat, in which condition it remained until Matthew T. Brennan was appointed by the governor and senate to take office on March 1, 1868 as the successor of Mr. Bergen who had died on July 18, 1867. The political equilibrium of the board was thus re-established.

An Act passed April 25, 1864, entitled an Act to amend an Act passed April 15, 1857, and an Act passed April 10, 1860, provided that the unexplained absence, without leave, of any member of the Metropolitan Police who for five days should absent himself without leave, should be deemed and held to be a resignation by such member and be accepted as such.

The Act also established the following officers: treasurer's bookkeeper, secretary to the president, chief clerk, first deputy clerk, and deputy clerks not exceeding ten, surgeons not exceeding ten, and a drill captain. The superintendent and each captain, the law declared, should possess powers of general police supervision and inspection over all licensed or unlicensed pawnbrokers, venders, junk-shops, junk-boatmen, cartmen, dealers in second- hand merchandise, and auctioneers within the district. In like manner, gaming houses, where there were wagers of money at games of chance and the sale of lottery tickets were brought under the jurisdiction of the police for inspection. The superintendent could authorize any member of the force to enter the gaming house and arrest all persons found breaking the law.

The selling of liquor on the Sabbath, or on election day, was also prohibited, under a penalty of fifty dollars for each offence. It was made a misdemeanor, punishable by imprisonment not less than one year nor exceeding two years, or a fine not less than two hundred and fifty dollars, to use personal violence upon any elector on election day. The Board of Police were empowered to appoint all poll clerks.

That portion of the Metropolitan Police District consisting of the cities of New York and Brooklyn were divided into two inspection districts, surgeons districts, and precincts. The precincts were divided into patrolmen's beats or posts. The police force was divided into four divisions, and an inspector was assigned to the command of a division, and in case of riot or any other cause, when the force was called out in a body, he had command over the division to which he was assigned.

The First Division was under the command of Inspector Folk, and comprised the whole force of Brooklyn, including the sanitary squad and Atlantic Dock Police. The Second Division was under the command of Inspector Leonard, and comprised the First, Second, Third, Fifth, Eighth, Ninth, Fifteenth, Twenty sixth, Twenty- seventh and Twenty eighth Precincts of New York City, and Second Police Court Squad.

The Third Division was under the command of Inspector Carpenter, and comprised the Fourth, Sixth, Seventh, Tenth, Eleventh,

Thirteenth, Fourteenth, Seventeenth and Twenty- fifth Precincts of New York City, the First and Third Police Court Squads, and the Sanitary Company.

The Fourth Division was under the command of Inspector Dilks, and comprised the Twelfth, Sixteenth, Eighteenth, Nineteenth, Twentieth, Twenty first, Twenty- second, Twenty third, Twenty ninth, Thirtieth, Thirty first, Thirty second, Thirty second sub-precinct, and Thirty third Precincts of New York City, and the Fourth Police Court Squad.

The commissioners of the Metropolitan Police and the comptrollers of the cities of New York and Brooklyn convened as a Board of Estimate and Apportionment, annually, on or before July 1, and made up a financial estimate of the sums required for the ensuing year. The estimate was then submitted to a committee of revision, composed of the presidents respectively of the board of supervisors of the counties of New York, Kings, Westchester and Richmond, and of the Board of Aldermen of Brooklyn and the respective towns of Newtown, Flushing, and Jamaica in the county of Queens. If objection to the estimate was made, it became the duty of the Board of Estimate and Apportionment to consider and revise the same, such action being final.

No member of the force was permitted to accept for his own benefit, or share in, any present, gift, or reward. The Board, however, could permit any member to accept such gift or present for any extraordinary service rendered.

Patrolmen in the regular routine of duty, passed over every portion of the graded streets of the city each hour of the day and night, and in the thickly settled streets much more frequently. It was their duty to become acquainted with every tenement on their respective beats, and to familiarize themselves with the habits, business, and characters of the permanent inhabitants. At that time, robbery, burglary, and larceny were pursued by a large class of the criminal element. The impossibility of completely stopping these offenses should not prevent the patrolmen from making honest and earnest efforts to make those operations neither safe nor profitable. The professional thief seemed to have preserved the same traits through all ages. He was not ashamed of his profession, nor did the law possess sufficient terrors to exert a restraining influence, so long as detection was difficult and conviction uncertain.

As the Metropolitan Police entered 1866, the force consisted of:

33 Captains

179 Sergeants

1,772 Patrolmen

63 Doormen

2,047 Total

The legislature, on February 28, 1866, passed an Act to amend an Act passed April 25, 1864, to amend an Act passed April 15, 1857, and an Act passed April 10, 1860, to the following effect: To the County of Richmond there were apportioned one captain, two sergeants, and twenty-five men. Any part of any town adjoining the city of Brooklyn might be set apart by the Board of Supervisors of the county of Kings for the purpose of having a patrol force. The expenses at tending this police force were levied and collected in the annual taxes of said district.

Yonkers and West Farms, in Westchester County had, by a vote of town meetings, respectively authorized a permanent police, and made the required fiscal arrangements. Yonkers authorized a force of fourteen, and West Farms a force of six men. In each town a portion of the police did duty as horse patrol, which greatly increased their efficiency.

The force in West Farms entered upon their duties on January 13th, 1866; in Richmond County on June 16th, and in Yonkers on August 10th. The town of West Farms constituted a sub-station of the Thirty-second Precinct, with a sergeant in command. The station house at

Tremont, Richmond County, was constituted a precinct designated as the Fifty-first Precinct. The station house was in the village of Stapleton. The town of Yonkers was constituted a sub-station of the Thirty second Precinct, designated as Yonkers sub-station, with a station house in the village of Yonkers. The Tremont and Yonkers sub-stations were under the command of the captain of the Thirty-second Precinct.

The only interest in obtaining a regular contingent of police in Queens was expressed on January 28th, 1870, when a town meeting was held in Newtown to let the people voice their opinion on bringing a Metropolitan Police precinct to Newtown and the costs involved. The issue soon became a moot point.

The amount of lost time by sickness and injuries during 1866 exceeded the amount of the preceding year by 311-days. The question of pay for lost time was one that was a controversial topic for the Board of Commissioners. Policemen were human, and so they, like the rest of the population, were subject to those physical infirmities of the flesh. No doubt much of those sporadic diseases were the result of natural causes and not to be avoided, while others were malingering, without a doubt. For the remainder of the existence of the Metropolitan Police, the commissioners continued to struggle with the paid sick leave policy and a method to identify malingering.

Brooklyn, in 1866 had only 307 patrolmen, which was less than 1 to 1,200 of the population. Its territory requiring police surveillance was equal to New York. This great extent of territory was divided into ten precincts, each of large extent. The extremes of the precinct were so remote from the respective station houses that it consumed a large portion of the policeman's time on patrol just going to and returning from their tours of duty. The commissioners contended that the law should be amended to allow the division of the territory of Brooklyn into a larger number of precincts, and that the welfare of the city demanded a considerable increase in the number of Patrolmen.

During the year 1867, 1,112 candidates for appointment on the police force presented themselves for medical examination of which 503 were accepted as eligible for appointment. The quota of Policemen for the County of New York was placed at 1,800, and such additional number as the Board of Police, from time to time, should determine, not, however, to exceed 2,000 thousand men.

The Act of April 25, 1867 (Chapter 806) established a central office in the City of New York, to be known as " the Central Department of the Metropolitan Police, " and in Brooklyn to be known as " the Office of Inspector of Metropolitan Police."

John G. Bergen, one of the commissioners of the Metropolitan Police, died on July 18th, 1867. His death was a serious loss to his associates and to the public service. The vacancy caused by Bergen's death was filled by the legislature on February 12, 1868, by the appointment of Matthew T. Brennan. The Board then consisted of Thomas C. Acton, Joseph S. Bosworth, Benjamin F. Manierre, and Matthew T. Brennan.

During 1868, the station house and prison accommodations for the use of the police force were considerably improved. In the Tenth Precinct, the new station house and prison on Eldridge Street were completed and occupied. In the Eighth, Twenty-first and Thirty-second Precincts, the buildings were completed and occupied. The station house in the Fifth Precinct on Leonard Street, was in course of construction. A contract had been awarded to enlarge and repair the station house and prison of the Third Precinct. The Seventh Precinct had been renovated and in the Twentieth Precinct Station House a contract had been awarded for the erection of a prison and lodgers' rooms in a separate building in the rear of the station house.

By Act of the legislature, April 27, 1869, the term of each commissioner of the Metropolitan Police was made to consist of eight years. By Act of May 12, 1869, the police commissioners of the

Metropolitan District were entitled to receive a salary of three thousand dollars in addition to their regular salary.

The Board of Metropolitan Police was re-organized in 1869. Mr. Thomas C. Acton, after nine years of honorable service, resigned, and on the same day, April 29th, Mr. Henry Smith was duly elected in his place. At a meeting of the commissioners, held on May 19, 1869, Joseph S. Bosworth was selected to act as president of the board. Commissioner Brennan tendered his resignation as treasurer, which was accepted, to take effect on June 5th, whereupon Henry Smith was selected to be treasurer of police, on and after the date of Mr. Brennan's resignation.

During 1869 patrolmen in New York City numbered 2,000, or 1 patrolman for every 500 residents. In Brooklyn the number of patrolmen was 368, or about 1 patrolman for every 1,000 residents.

The length of open streets and piers in New York demanding patrol service was over 450-miles, and in Brooklyn at least 350-miles. In New York, the average length of night posts was sixty-three one hundredths of a mile, and day tours over a mile and a quarter; while in Brooklyn the average length of night posts was two and fifty-four one-hundredth miles, and day posts five and eight one-hundredth miles. In each city there were posts of even greater length.

Owing to necessary to concentrate the force in the more densely populated districts of both cities, the coverage of the night posts was such that the policeman's call could not be heard from the center to the extremes of the posts, while in Brooklyn the patrolmen were so far apart that they were not within supporting distance of each other.

During 1869, a report of the board of surgeons reflected that that the amount of time lost by sickness and injuries in the whole force was 22,764 days. Payment of salary was allowed for 13,116 days, and payment of salary was disallowed for 9,647 days. Though the number of the police force was greater than in the preceding year, the amount of time lost by sickness was considerably less.

Even though the police force sick record had improved, it was still a serious item in the public expenditure and represented a sum more than equal to the combined salary of thirty-five patrolmen. The reduction in the proportion of sick time was attributed by the Board in some degree, by the members who were broken down in health being induced to resign and accept pensions. The improved sanitary condition of the station houses, also, it was believed, contributed to improve the health of the force.

At the conclusion of 1869 the breakdown of the Metropolitan Police was as follows:

34 Captains

131 Sergeants

1,994 Patrolmen

73 Doormen

2,232 Total,

This number was inclusive of personnel performing duty in the court squad, sanitary squad, detective squad, special details, and the house of detention.

The number of precincts was thirty-two, their designation being by number. The number of men authorized by law was:

2,000 New York

368 Brooklyn

26 Richmond County

14 Yonkers

8 West Farms

2,416 Total

When the organization of the force was established with a superintendent and four inspectors, the number of patrolmen was limited to 1,600. Since then, from time to time, the force was increased more than fifty per cent by adding 816 patrolmen, and a proportionate number of captains, sergeants, and doormen.

It has been asserted that the Metropolitan Police system was the best ever devised and produced more satisfactory results than any of its predecessors. This, after all, is not very great praise, as, properly speaking, New York previously had no police force worthy of the name, with all lacking in that efficiency and esprit de corps which sprang from discipline, organization and the soldierly instinct produced by the wearing of a uniform. The Metropolitans, however, were being educated in the practical school of a policeman, and the results were beginning to be felt and appreciated. In all important characteristics, the Metropolitan Police were undoubtedly superior to their predecessors. "Progress" was the watchword, but just how far the Metropolitan policing system would have progressed was never to be known because the police department was about to enter another era of re-organization and development.

Issued to the Metropolitan Police after the Draft Riot

Captain George Washington Walling

The Metropolitan Police that fought with, and then replaced, the Municipal Police, c.1860. *New York City Police Department*

CHAPTER 7: THE LAST INNING FOR THE METS

On April 5, 1870, there was passed an Act to re- organize the local government of the City of New York. This charter is commonly known as the "Tweed Charter." By it, the police board was made to consist of four Commissioners, who were appointed for the respective terms of eight, seven, six, and five years. The Act also wrested control of the police department away from the state and returned it to the New York City municipal government. To better understand the reason for the demise of the Metropolitan Police we have to take a look at one of the most influential and infamous names in New York City politics.

New York City was not a pretty sight after the Civil War. The city's unpaved streets were strewn with trash thrown from windows and horse manure from animals pulling carriages. Black smoke clogged the air, wafted from the burning coal and wood that heated homes and powered factories. Diseases like cholera and tuberculosis thrived in the unhealthy environment. More than one million people were crowded into the city, many in dilapidated tenements. Poverty, illiteracy, crime, and vice were rampant problems for the poor, and for the Irish and German immigrants who made up almost half the population. The city government offered a very few basic services to alleviate the suffering, and churches and private charities were often overwhelmed by the needy. One politician who discovered how to provide these services stepped forward to initiate vast improvements to the city. The problem was that he wanted a lot in return.

One of the most important figures of 19th century New York City was William Tweed, also known as Boss Tweed. On one hand, Tweed was responsible for improving the infrastructure that allowed the city to grow, such as the water and sewer systems. On the other hand, he was one of the most corrupt politicians ever to rise to power in the United States.

Tweed was born in New York on April 3, 1823. After establishing himself as a charismatic and street-smart figure in his Manhattan neighborhood, he kicked off his political career with a successful campaign for alderman of the Seventh Ward in 1852. By 1853 Tweed had a seat in the United States House of Representatives. Life in Washington D.C. didn't suit him, and he headed back to the city after only one term. In 1856 Tweed landed a position on the city's new Board of Supervisors, and from there he never looked back.

Tammany Hall was founded in the 1780s and was originally meant to be a fraternal society where like-minded individuals could get together and talk about politics. Their actions became increasingly political as the decades went on and by the 1840s, they had firmly established themselves as an arm of the Democratic party. Even more importantly, Tammany had developed a deep connection with the city's growing population of immigrants, particularly the Irish. Tammany Hall helped countless new arrivals get jobs, set up lives, and even achieve U.S. citizenship. In return Tammany got votes for candidates they put up in elections across the city. Tammany Hall always had a bit of a stink about it, but despite the air of corruption, they kept growing in political influence, and in 1868 Tweed became head of Tammany Hall and was elected to the New York Senate.

While Tweed was serving in the House of Representatives, he had made friends across party lines. These relationships, along with some well-placed bribes allowed the passage of what came to be known as the "Tweed Charter," in 1870, which undid the New York State takeover of 1857 and brought all of the city's infrastructure, including the treasury, under the control of the city municipal government and Tweed. While Tweed was mostly concerned about getting control of the city's money, another consequence of the Tweed Charter was that the Metropolitan Police District was dissolved with policing in the city returning to a

Municipal Police Department under the direct control of the mayor and municipal authorities.

Tweed's campaign of plundering in the city went on for a few more years In 1871, fortune stopped smiling on Boss Tweed, and the person most responsible for his downfall was a cartoonist working for Harper's Weekly named Thomas Nast. Nast initiated a campaign to reveal Tweed's corruption in a way that the thousands of New York residents who were illiterate could understand – cartoons.

On July 18, 1871, Nast and his colleagues at the New York Times who were also after Tweed's scalp, were given a gift. One of Tweed's lieutenants named Jimmy O'Brien believed he was being swindled out of his rightful share of the graft, so he made duplicates of all the city's financial records and calmly strolled into the Times building and handed them to an editor. Before the Times received the records to document Tweed's corrupt activities, Nast's cartoons were humorous personal attacks, because, ultimately, he couldn't prove anything. When Nast started incorporating the theme of the documented corruption in his cartoons, Tweed knew he had a problem. He summed up his situation by stating, "I don't care a straw for your newspaper articles. My constituents don't know how to read, but they can't help seeing them damn pictures." It was all downhill from there. Tweed was arrested in October 1871 and the next couple of years would consist of a series of trials until Tweed was finally convicted of 204 charges in 1873 and sentenced to 12-years, a sentence quickly reduced to 1-year. When his year was up, Tweed was brought up on civil charges and when he wasn't able to make bail he was sent back to jail. Jail for Tweed was a two-bedroom set of rooms with a library and his own personal aide. He was even permitted out for carriage rides in Central Park. It was during one of these rides in 1875 that he escaped to New Jersey where he boarded a boat that ended up in Cuba and six weeks later Tweed disembarked in Spain. Very quickly, however, he was recognized in Spain (from Nast's cartoons,) and sent back to jail in New York City where he died in 1878, a broken, penniless man.

An ironic twist to the Tweed saga was that it was the New York City Municipal Police in 1871 who arrested Tweed. This was the same Municipal Police that Tweed was responsible for bringing back when the Tweed Charter dissolved the Metropolitan Police.

At the time the Act of April 5, 1870, To re-organize the local government of the City of New York, went into effect, every person connected with the Metropolitan Police Department was transferred to the new Municipal Police Department and continued in the office which he held at the time of such transfer. On April 11th the Board was organized by the election of Joseph S. Bosworth as President, Matthew T. Brennan as Treasurer, and the appointment of Seth C. Hawley as Chief Clerk. Mr. Brennan resigned his office on October 7th and Henry Smith was thereupon elected Treasurer.

On April 11, 1870, John A. Kennedy, who had been superintendent of the Metropolitan Police from May 23, 1860 until he was transferred to the Municipal Police Department, resigned his office. The vacancy created thereby was filled by appointing as superintendent John Jourdan, then Captain of the Sixth Precinct. Superintendent Jourdan died on October 10, 1870, and on October 17th, James J. Kelso, captain of the detective force, was appointed superintendent of police.

And just like that the Metropolitan Police, which over a period of thirteen years had grown into a professional, prideful organization, was gone, falling victim to the scourge of the era - politics.

Throughout the life of the Metropolitan Police, the changes in the subordinates of the force were much fewer than among the commissioners. Mr. Kennedy had been superintendent continuously since 1860. Mr. Seth C. Hawley, who was appointed by President Grant Collector of Internal Revenue for the Eighth District in March of 1870 had been Chief Clerk since the summer of 1860. Throughout the force good behavior had regulated the tenure of office, and the inspectors and captains remained almost unchanged, except by deaths and resignations, and there were many captains who held their positions during the entire lifespan of the Metropolitan Police. As a result of maintaining a force of senior officers and patrolmen who did not have to worry about annual re-appointments, the force moved beyond the machinations of the mere politicians to such an extent that it had reached a higher standard than would have been possible had the board been at liberty to appoint and dismiss members, as political considerations might demand.

There was a feeling by many, however, that the new law was forcing the police department to take a big step backwards by giving the five commissioners, to be appointed by the mayor and aldermen, power to remove any and every member of the police force without any cause whatsoever, except their pleasure. The fear was that the captains and sergeants who took actions against the interests of city politicians during the existence of the Metropolitan policing system, would be removed by the new regime, including all the precinct commanders.

As the curtain fell on the comparative order and decency that the New York "Mets" had brought out of the riotous beginning of the decade, was the anxiety and apprehension expressed by the mainly Republican segment of the city warranted? Maybe. Moving forward from 1870 the police department continued to struggle under political influences, and it still does today. But what evolved from the era of the Metropolitans was the NYPD, a department that is far from perfect, but as articulated by George Matsell, represents New York's Finest.

The Metropolitan Police in 1870

John Jourdan

Superintendent Kelso.

JOHN S. FOLK.

Tweed in 1870

One of Thomas Nast's cartoons that led to Tweed's downfall

CHAPTER 8: HEROES

One of the grim realities of policing is the fact that there will always be police officers who make the supreme sacrifice in performing their duty to protect the citizenry. This reality was no different for the Metropolitan Police Department. The following is a list of the heroes who gave their lives in the line of duty during the existence of the Metropolitan Police Department.

THOMAS SPARKS – 7/4/1857

Patrolman Sparks succumbed to injuries received when he was struck by an object after arresting a man for assault. Sparks had been appointed a special patrolman only one night before due to rioting going on in the city. Two rival gangs, "The Bowery Boys" and "The Dead Rabbits" had faced off against each other.

Patrolman Sparks heard a cry for help and responded and made an arrest. As Sparks was walking the arrested subject toward White Street, he was struck with an object by a member of the "Dead Rabbits" gang. He was taken home where his condition deteriorated. He died five days after being assaulted.

EUGENE ANDERSON – 7/20/1857

Patrolman Anderson was shot during a burglary near the corner of Grand Street and Centre Street in Manhattan. While on patrol duty Anderson was drawn to the calls of "stop thief". As he approached the location the suspect drew a horse pistol and fired five shots, killing him.

A second patrolman and a civilian arrived on the scene and the patrolman ordered the civilian to chase the suspect while he attended to Patrolman Anderson. The civilian met up with another patrolman and chased the suspect for several blocks before capturing him inside a building at 120 Worth Street.

HORATIO SANGER 11/22/1857

Patrolman Horatio Sanger was killed when he was hit in the head by his own nightstick by a suspect he was arresting. Sanger had responded to a disturbance on Bleeker Street and was arresting a suspect when that suspect took Sanger's nightstick and struck him in the head with it killing him instantly. The suspect was later arrested by other officers.

Patrolman Sanger was assigned to the 9th Precinct, the present-day 6th Precinct.

JOHN STEWARD 12/20/1859

Patrolman Steward was killed in the collapse of a building at 54 and 56 Broad Street in Manhattan. Steward and several other patrolmen responded to the address after much of the building collapsed. Patrolman Steward was assigned a post near the front of the building. After taking his post the rest of the building collapsed, seriously injuring Steward and killing a civilian. Steward was removed to City Hospital where he died later that day from his injury. He was survived by a wife, two daughters and a son

DAVID MARTIN 8/6/1861

Patrolman David Martin was stabbed to death while attempting to arrest a suspect that had just burglarized 128 Adams Street in Brooklyn. When a neighbor heard someone in the house, he summoned Patrolman Martin. Martin gave chase as he fled south on Pearl Street. He overtook the suspect at the corner of Prospect Street and Washington Street. As Martin grabbed hold of the suspect, the suspect suddenly turned and stabbed Patrolman Martin twice in the neck. Although gravely wounded, Martin was able to hit the suspect in the head with his club, knocking him senseless to the sidewalk. Two patrolmen who heard the disturbance responded and captured the suspect. Patrolman Martin was removed to a doctor's office, but the doctor was unable to treat the wounds and Martin died 15 minutes later.

Patrolman Martin was assigned to the 2nd Precinct, the present day 84th Precinct. He was survived by his wife and three children.

HENRY L. WILLIAMS 10/14/1862

Patrolman Henry Williams was shot and killed while attempting to arrest an intoxicated man who was harassing a female in front of 142 Charles Street shortly after 10PM. While on foot patrol Patrolman Williams heard the woman asking the man to leave her alone. He approached the man and instructed him to leave. As the man was walking away, he tripped over a cart in the roadway. Williams decided to arrest the man for being intoxicated. As he grabbed hold of the suspect, the suspect turned and shot Patrolman Williams in the lower abdomen. A nearby officer answered Williams' screams for help and arrested the suspect. Several citizens took Williams to his home and called a doctor. The doctor was unable to remove the bullet, and Patrolman Williams succumbed to his wound two days later.

Patrolman Williams served with the New York Metropolitan Police Force for seven years and was assigned to the 9th Precinct, the present-day 6th Precinct. His wife and three children survived him.

EDWARD DIPPEL 7/19/1863

Patrolman Edward Dippel succumbed to a gunshot wound sustained while resisting rioters angry over President Abraham Lincoln's Civil War Draft. Officer Dippel attempted to stop rioters from looting an establishment when he was shot.

Patrolman Dipple served with the Metropolitan Police Department for two years and was assigned to the Broadway Squad. He is survived by his wife and daughter.

PETER MCINTYRE 8/9/1863

Patrolman McIntyre was violently beaten with an iron pipe by a group of men protesting the Civil War Draft, while performing riot duty at 3rd Avenue and 46th street in Manhattan. He was removed to Bellevue Hospital where he died almost a month later from his injuries.

JOHN T. VAN BUREN 11/7/1863

Patrolman Van Buren was violently beaten by a group of men protesting the Civil War Draft, while performing riot duty at 3rd

Avenue and 46th street in Manhattan. Patrolman Van Buren died four months later from his injuries.

Patrolman Van Buren was assigned to the 8th precinct, the present-day 17th Precinct.

JOHN STARKEY 1/20/1864

Patrolman John Starkey was violently assaulted and beaten during the Civil War draft riots. He died from his injuries seven months later.

Patrolman Starkey was assigned to the Central Office.

AUSTIN H. EASTERBROOK 2/6/1864

Patrolman Austin Easterbrook died of injuries he received while trying to stop a runaway horse. A pair of horses attached to a horse drawn buggy were frightened and broke loose on Broadway near 14th Street in Manhattan. Patrolman Easterbrook attempted to stop the horses before they injured anyone. While attempting to do this, Easterbrook was severely injured. He was removed to the hospital, where he died eight days later from his injuries.

Patrolman Easterbrook was assigned to what is the present day 25th Precinct.

GEORGE W. DURYEA 5/16/1864

Patrolman George Duryea was shot and killed at the intersection of 2nd Avenue and 62nd Street while assisting in the arrest of a gang of thieves who had been operating in the area. Duryea was pursuing the suspects on foot when one of the suspects turned and fired two shots from a revolver. One of the shots struck Patrolman Duryea in the head, killing him instantly. The suspects fled the scene. One of the fleeing suspects was captured by another patrolman and a crowd of civilians who had come to the aid of the police. The suspect who murdered Patrolman Duryea was able to escape. He was never identified.

Patrolman Duryea served with the New York Metropolitan Police Department for 11 years and was assigned to the 19th Precinct, the present-day 17th Precinct. He was survived by his wife and seven children.

JOHN J. O'BRIEN 8/25/1864

Patrolman John O'Brien was shot and killed when he attempted to arrest a wanted fugitive. Patrolman O'Brien spotted the suspect as he walked his beat. He pursued the suspect into a liquor store at the corner of 41st Street and 8th Avenue and attempted to arrest him. The suspect drew a pistol and shot Patrolman O'Brien in the head. Although wounded, O'Brien pursued the suspect to 40th Street, where he collapsed from loss of blood. Patrolman O'Brien was removed to the hospital where he died four days later from his wounds. The suspect was apprehended 14 years later and charged with murder.

Patrolman O'Brien was assigned to the 17th Precinct. He was survived by his wife and two children and is buried in Brooklyn, New York.

CHARLES CURRAN 10/6/1864

Patrolman Charles Curran was shot and killed while attempting to arrest a man while responding to a shooting at the Democratic Club during a meeting in Brooklyn's 5th Ward. The suspect fled the scene and encountered Patrolman Curran who was responding to the scene. The suspect shot Curran in the head, causing the fatal injury. The suspect attempted to flee again but was captured.

Patrolman Curran had served with the New York Metropolitan Police Force for eight years and was assigned to the 42nd Precinct, the present-day 84th Precinct. He was survived by his wife, four sons, and daughter.

JOSEPH NULETT 11/7/1864

Patrolman Joseph Nulett was shot and killed by a suspect he had just arrested. Patrolman Nulett was called to 77 West 24th Street in Manhattan by a woman. When he arrived the observed two men attempting to break the window shutters to the building. He told both men to leave, but one of the men refused. Patrolman Nulett placed that suspect under arrest and began to escort him back to the station house. While walking back on 29th Street, between Broadway and Fifth Avenue, the suspect drew a pistol and killed Patrolman Nulett.

Patrolman Nulett was assigned to the 29th Precinct, the present-day 10th Precinct. He was survived by his wife and two children.

THOMAS WALKER 8/15/1865

Patrolman Thomas Walker was shot and killed when he and his partner responded to a woman's cry for help at 95 Seventh Avenue in Manhattan. A group of men had just raped the woman. Patrolman Walker and his partner approached the locked door and Walker called out to the suspects "We are officers, you villains! What are you doing to this woman?" Patrolman Walker's partner then attempted to pull the door open, but at the same time some of the suspects pushed the door open and ran. One suspect, still inside the building fired out the open door, killing Patrolman Walker. The suspect then fled on foot with Walker's partner in pursuit. Walker's partner fired three times at the fleeing suspects before his revolver jammed. While on 16th Street, about 150 feet east of Seventh Avenue, the suspect threw down his hat and coat and hid behind a tree-box. The suspect was arrested by Patrolman Walker's partner, and a coroner's inquest found that the apprehended suspect was responsible for firing the fatal shot at Patrolman Walker. The other eight suspects escaped but were arrested as accomplices to Walker's murder. The shooter was found guilty of manslaughter in the Court of General Sessions on December 18th, 1865.

Patrolman Walker was assigned to the 29th Precinct and was survived by his wife and young daughter.

ROBERT S. MCCHESNEY 10/19/1867

Patrolman Robert McChesney was stabbed and killed as he attempted to arrest a intoxicated prostitute who was insulting pedestrians. When McChesney placed his hand on the suspect, she turned quickly and stabbed him in the neck with a three bladed knife.

Patrolman McChesney fell to the ground, but was able give the alarm rap, calling several patrolmen to the scene. The first patrolman to arrive arrested the suspect after a struggle in which she attempted to stab him. Two other responding patrolmen carried McChesney to the hospital where he died.

Patrolman McChesney served with the New York Metropolitan Police force for just two months and seven days. He was assigned to the 8th Precinct, the present- day 1st Precinct.

Patrolman McChesney was survived by his wife.

CHARLES THOMPSON 12/1/1867

Patrolman Thompson succumbed to wounds received one month earlier when he was stabbed while trying to arrest a drunk man. The suspect was causing a disturbance in a grocery store on James Street when Thompson attempted to arrest him. The suspect fled into an alley and stabbed Patrolman Thompson in the shoulder. The suspect was apprehended.

Patrolman Thompson was assigned to the 4th Precinct, the present-day 5th Precinct

HENRY CORBETT 7/13/1868

Patrolman Henry Corbett drowned in the North River while attempting to rescue a 14-year-old girl who had just fallen overboard from a barge attached to the steamer "Seth Low." The ship tried to dock the party excursion barge at 152nd Street so the passengers could disembark. Patrolman Corbett was assisting the passengers off the barge when the steamer pulled away from the dock, causing him and several passengers to fall in. Patrolman Corbett's body was recovered near 96th Street several days later. The girl he was attempting to rescue also drowned. The captain of the "Seth Low" was held on charges of criminal neglect.

Patrolman Corbett had served with the Metropolitan Police Force for eight years and was assigned to the 32nd Precinct of the Metropolitan Police Force, an area now covered by the 30th Precinct of the New York City Police Department. He was survived by his wife and five children.

JOHN SMEDICK 7/23/1868

Patrolman John Smedick was shot and killed after being ambushed by a career criminal near the intersection of 1st Avenue and 32nd Street, Manhattan.

Patrolman Smedick was on foot patrol when he was approached by the suspect. Without warning, the suspect shot Smedick in the chest. When Smedick fell to the ground, the suspect fired again, striking Patrolman Smedick in the head. A nearby patrolman heard the shots and responded. He chased the suspect on foot while exchanging shots. The suspect was arrested and charged with murder. He was executed by hanging in 1870.

Patrolman Smedick had served with New York Metropolitan Police Force for five years and had been assigned to the 21st Precinct. He was survived by his wife and two children.

JOHN A. BRANAGAN 8/10/1869

Patrolman Branagan died of injuries he received while assisting with backing out a horse drawn lumber truck from a ferry yard. Branagan was on his post at the Hamilton Ferry and as the truck was backing out, the horses changed direction, causing the load of lumber to fall from the truck onto Branagan. He was severely injured and was taken to his residence and the coroner was summoned. Patrolman Branagan died shortly thereafter from his injuries.

Patrolman Branagan had served with the New York City Police Department for 12 and a half years and was survived by his wife and four children.

PHILLIP LAMBRECK 3/14/1872

Detective Lambreck died of injuries he received several weeks earlier when he was assaulted by a gang of notorious ruffians at the corner of 59th Street and First Avenue in Manhattan. A Patrolman from the 19th Precinct was on patrol on First Avenue when he was called to 883 First Avenue to quell a disturbance at a saloon. When the patrolman entered, he was nearly killed by the disorderly crowd.

Detective Lambreck his roundsman and another patrolman, all in civilian clothes, responded to the location in an attempt to locate the suspect who had fled. As they were searching, they came across a group of six drunk men at the corner of 59th Street and 2nd Avenue. The group of men attacked the officers. Detective Lambreck drew his revolver and fired one shot at the men. One of the men then picked up a large slab of marble and struck Detective Lambreck on the back of the head, fracturing his skull. Other officers responded to the scene and were able to take the suspects into custody. Patrolman Lambreck was taken to St. Luke's Hospital, where he remained until his death three weeks later.

The suspect who struck Detective Lambreck was later convicted of second-degree murder.

Detective Lambreck was assigned to the 19th Precinct, the present-day 17th Precinct. He is buried in Calvary Cemetery, in Woodside, Queens County, New York.

EPILOGUE

As a kid growing up in Jackson Heights, Queens, New York City during the 1960s, like most boys of the era, I had a passion for baseball cards. For a period of time during adulthood I collected baseball cards and kept my cards in pristine, mint condition by delicately placing the rectangular pieces of cardboard in protective plastic sleeves. I eventually tired of the hobby because there were just too many companies producing cards and too many sets being produced by each company. Things were so much simpler when I was a kid.

I could care less about keeping my Topps baseball cards in mint condition when I brought them to school and spent hours flipping them and playing the games of "Letters" and "Colors" in Our lady of Fatima's schoolyard. As a New York City kid, it was always a thrill to open a pack and find the cards of players from the Yankees or Mets inside.

The Mets began appearing on cards when the team came into existence in 1962, but few people realize that the Mets I have written about in this book – the Metropolitan Police, appeared on trading cards back in the 19th century.

Beginning in 1875, cards depicting actresses, baseball players, Native American chiefs, boxers, national flags, and wild animals were issued by the U.S.-based Allen & Ginter tobacco company. These are considered to be some of the first cigarette cards. Other tobacco companies soon followed suit.

Each set of cards typically consisted of 25 or 50 related subjects, but series of over 100 cards per issue are known. Popular themes were 'beauties', usually famous actresses, film stars and models, and sports stars. In the U.S. the cards mainly featured baseball players, while in the rest of the world, football and cricket were featured. Nature, military heroes and uniforms, heraldry, locomotives, and city views were other card subjects.

The most famous tobacco card is the T206 baseball card produced by the American Tobacco company depicting the Pittsburgh Pirates Honus Wagner, known as "The Flying Dutchman," a dead-ball era baseball player who is widely considered to be one of the best players of all time. The card was issued from 1909 to 1911 as part of itsT206 series. Wagner refused to allow production of his baseball card to continue, either because he did not want children to buy cigarette packs to get his card, or because he wanted more compensation from the ATC. The ATC ended production of the Wagner card, and a total of only 50 to 200 cards were ever distributed to the public. The exact number is unknown. In 2016 the card sold for $3,120,000.

Baseball players, actresses, flags and wild animals were just few of the subjects to be featured on tobacco cards. I was amazed to learn that there had been a set of tobacco cards featuring the New York Mets. Let me clarify - these cards do not contain the images of Mets baseball players. This set of Mets cards depicts the Metropolitan Police. Buchner "Police Inspectors & Captains and Chiefs of the Fire Departments" series (N288). Issued in 1887 by D. Buchner & Co. included. 97 unnumbered The front of each card contained the image of a police captain or inspector, while on the back was printed: WE WILL PACK IN EVERY PACKAGE OF "ONE OF THE FINEST" TOBACCO THE PORTRAITS OF THE POLICE INSPECTORS & CAPTAINS IN UNIFORM.

Before you give my book a one-star review, let me clarify that I understand that these cards were produced in 1887, thirteen years after the Metropolitan Police Department was dissolved. I realize the cards are not a set of the "Metropolitan Police," but please allow me to take a little poetic license. Since the set includes only captains and inspectors, all of the officers had many years of experience and all were on the job during the era of the Metropolitan Police, some of them being prominently featured in this book.

This brings me to the end of the tale of the original New York Metropolitans – the Metropolitan Police Department. There's only one more thing left to say – "Let's Go Mets!" Hey, wait a minute, I'm a Yankees fan!

Capt. Wm. C.F. Berghold

Capt. Jno. J. Brogan

Capt. James Campbell

Patrick Campbell

The front of the cards

WE WILL PACK

IN EVERY PACKAGE OF

"ONE OF THE FINEST"

TOBACCO

THE PORTRAITS OF THE

POLICE INSPECTORS & CAPTAINS and CHIEFS of the FIRE DEPARTMENTS.

IN UNIFORM.

COPYRIGHTED 1887   JULIUS BIEN & CO. LITH.

The back side of the cards

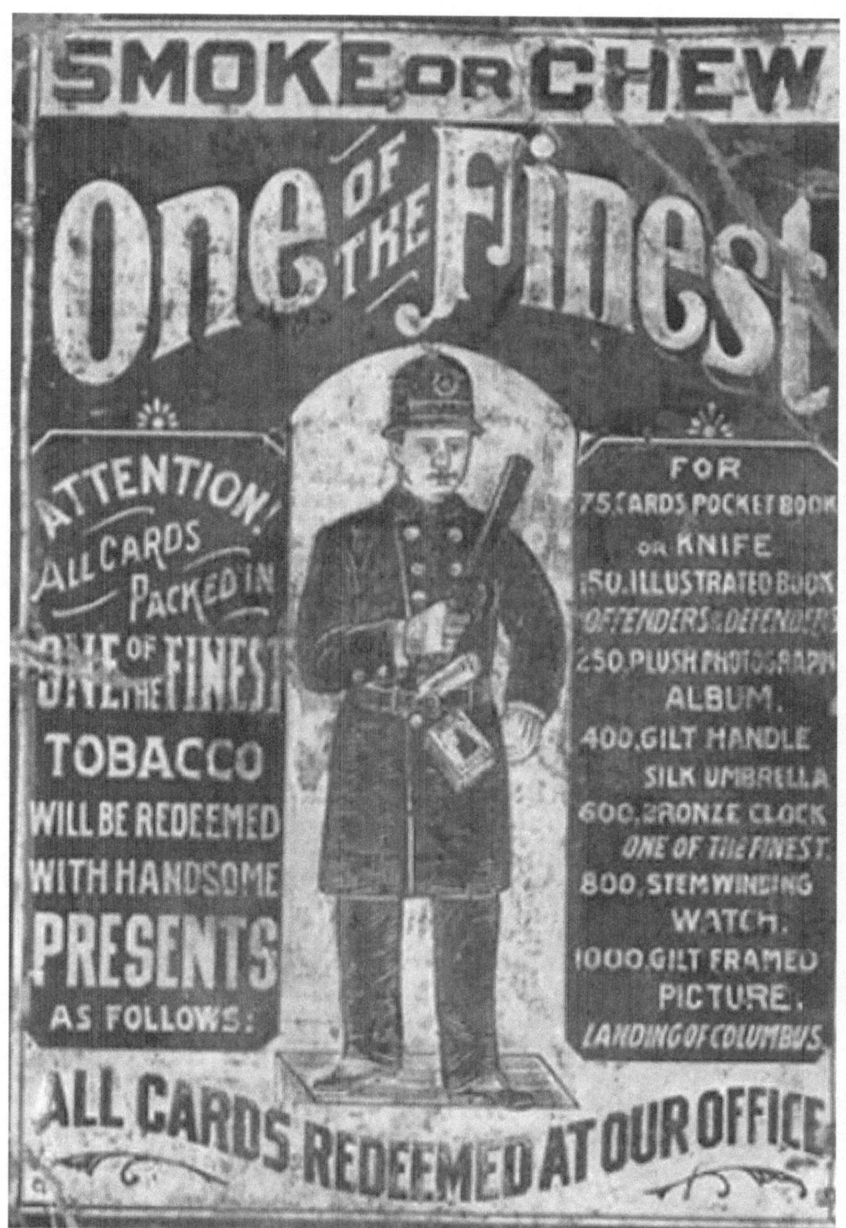

The poster used at tobacco shops to advertise the police cards.

www.ingramcontent.com/pod-product-compliance
Lightning Source LLC
Chambersburg PA
CBHW051214160726
47994CB00002B/603